Stand-by 4

Starting Points for Drama

Stand-by 4
Starting Points for Drama

Arthur Brittin

Designed and illustrated by
Barrie Richardson

ARNOLD - WHEATON

The Stand-by series includes:

Stand-by   A miscellany of unexpected lessons
Stand-by 2   Fun with basic skills
Stand-by 3   Early Art and Craft
Stand-by 4   Starting Points for Drama

Arnold-Wheaton
A Division of E. J. Arnold & Son Limited
Parkside Lane, Leeds, LS11 5TD

A member of the Pergamon Group
Headington Hill Hall, Oxford, OX3 0BW

ISBN 0·560·03497·0

Copyright © **Arthur Brittin** 1987

First published 1987

Printed in Great Britain by A. Wheaton & Co. Ltd.,
Hennock Road, Exeter

Contents

Page

Introduction   8

Starters

Follow my leader   12
Instant rhymes   13
Echoes   14
Sounds like . . .   16
Now look here   17
Newspaper towers   18
Machinery   19
Games, games, games   20
Dislocated voices   22
Can you, do you, will you listen?   23
More sounds   24
Guess what?   26

Physicals

Obedient robot   27
Noughts and crosses   28
Making up the numbers   29
Pictures   30
The model   31
Mime sequences   32
Freeze-frame!   33
The games   34
Taking a walk   35
Puppets – a miscellany   38

Stories

Helpers   41
The tunnel folk   42
Rhymes and sayings   44
Nursery rhyme time   46
True or false?   47
Treasure!   48
The boy who cried wolf   50
Making pictures   52

Contents

Page

Questions and Answers

Charades	53
Our town	54
Who am I?	55
Nursery rhyme time again	56
Recollections	58
Possessions	60
Detection	62

Openings

Dialogues	64
Wild green jungle	66
Objects of interest	68
Superstitions	69
A view of the sea	70
Verse time	72
Emma's week	74
The numbers game	76
Holidays	78
Rumour	80
Survival	82

Decisions

Publications	83
The time box	84
Moving house	86
Neighbourhood matters	88
Reconstructions	92

Situations and Role-Play

Persuasion	94
Work places	96
Animation	98
Proverbs	99
What's it all about?	100
Complaints	102
The photograph	104
Crime and punishment	106

Contents

Page

Openings   **118**

Looking at . . .
Limericks and clerihews
Abstract themes
Magic and the supernatural
Costume
Material
Chorus
History based
Story based
Sound patterns
Voices

Decisions   **121**

Advertisements
The expert
Making plans
Applications
Rules
Special occasions
People who work for us
Health topics
The trial

Situations and role-plays **124**

Role-play
Coping
Starters (1)
Starters (2)
Imaginary environment
Let's be . . .
Script

Page

Starters   **110**

Pass it on
Port and starboard
Connections
Lucky dip
Optimist/pessimist
What you make it
The minister's cat
Leading

Physicals   **112**

Experiments with paper
Looking after . . .
Let's go
The senses
Forgotten games
Work songs
Mime tasks
The elements

Stories   **114**

Identification
Names
Dialect
Descriptions
Stories/telling
Stories/making up
Hesitation/repetition

Questions and Answers   **117**

Leadership
Who uses?
Who says?

Introduction

The Stand-by series contains a vast range of ideas and suggestions for Infant, Primary and Middle school classrooms, particularly designed for situations where time for preparation is limited. This book – Stand-by 4 – offers a wide variety of opportunities for drama, talk, language work and co-operation.

It is planned for times when a teacher has to take over a colleague's class with minimum notice, or when a school outing necessitates a re-jigging of groups. Experienced and less experienced teachers will find in these pages a wealth of possibilities for practical, enjoyable and educationally valuable activities. They are planned in detail, but never sufficiently cut and dried to prevent the class and the teacher from influencing the flow of events with their own ideas and imagination.

Each lesson is complete in itself, although the nature of the approach naturally throws up possibilities for extending the work. I have framed these possibilities as 'Further Steps', from which the teacher can choose, as appropriate.

The work is carefully structured so that teachers who have not used drama extensively can follow clear guidance; those who already use drama as a learning method should find fresh ideas for development.

For each lesson, we have suggested a minimum age and an approximate running time. These are offered merely as a guide, as there is ample evidence that a game designed for seven-year-olds can often work perfectly well for eleven-year-olds – indeed the reverse is sometimes true! A lesson that takes ten minutes today may take twenty minutes tomorrow. In all cases the teacher will be in the best position to assess the children's stage of development and readiness to cope.

The activities are grouped in eight sections. There is no
conceptual progression through the book, but each section
offers ways in to a certain type of work. It is possible to
concentrate on one section, or alternatively to offer the children
a wider range of experiences by spreading the choice; lessons
from two different sections can be combined into one sequence.
If the activity fits in with the established curriculum, so much
the better. It might, with advantage, supplement that work. It is
not meant to supplant it.

The lessons require varying degrees of preparation. In some
cases there is none at all. In other cases, resources are needed:
for example, card, paper, felt-tips, old newspapers. Most
teachers will have these on hand. In a few cases a larger space,
like the school hall, will help, but generally a normal classroom
will be fine.

Group co-operation in solving problems or carrying out tasks is
an important aspect, which is also developed through the direct
interchange of role-play. The teacher's involvement in role will
add a further dimension.

Finally, Section Eight is a wide-ranging bank of ideas
corresponding to the preceding seven sections. These are briefly
and concisely described with the aim that the teacher can
accept the idea and work on it in ways to suit the growing
needs of the class.

Materials

Most of these materials will already be available in the classroom, but several items are worth collecting. They are rarely essential for the activities in the book, but if you have them on hand, further possibilities are opened up.

Paper – various kinds and sizes

Pencils

Felt-tips – chunky and fine

Card

Chalk

Magazines ⎱ useful source of pictures, adverts,
Newspapers ⎰ portraits, etc.

Miscellaneous objects – alarm clock, fir cone, old camera, etc.

Items of costume – hats, scarves, etc. for emblematic costume.

Percussion instruments – these are fairly easy to make and once made can be used time and time again, e.g.:

Beans/pasta in containers

Musical bottles
– fill with varying levels of water to produce different notes. Arrange the bottles so the notes form a scale.

Drums
– cover empty containers with plastic film/carrier bag and secure with rubber band.
– for bongo drums cover different sized cardboard tubes tied together with string.
– for steel band use upturned cake tins, coke cans, etc.

Xylophone – made from wooden sticks or pieces of bamboo cut to different lengths.

Tambourine – cut holes in circular lid or yoghurt pot, thread string through holes adding milk-bottle tops where appropriate.

Cymbals – use old saucepan lids.

Making improvised sounds with yourself and your environment is of great value. Briefly these are the possibilities:

Vocal: These can be either recognisable words or sounds.

Yourself: The sounds you can make with parts of your own body: hands through hair, finger and thumb, clapping etc.

Yourself with an object: Fingers on jeans, breath on paper.

Object and object: Shoe sole on floor, pencil on comb.

This improvised use of sound accords much better with the purpose of this book, which is to provide support in an emergency with a minimum of preparation. It also introduces an element of experimentation.

It is hoped that, when the situation arises, this book will be a source of useful and usable ideas, and a stimulus to action which will be rewarding and fun.

FOLLOW MY LEADER

Age range: 6+

Time: 10 minutes

Aim: To enjoy a simple game

The class will be asked to 'Do what I do', so you can choose actions which the children can follow without moving from their desks (driving, ironing, throwing, catching, etc.). However, if you can make some floor space available then a greater range of movements can be covered. If there isn't enough room for the whole class to move around together, allocate teams, and move one team at a time.

1 Tell the children to follow your movements and actions as closely as possible. Start by saying 'Follow my leader' and/or 'Do what I do'. The children will follow.

2 All sorts of ideas should occur to you once you get warmed up. Don't forget, you can make all sorts of sounds as well as making all sorts of movements. Be completely non-judgemental.

3 Choose someone else to be leader and follow them. Encourage them to develop their own ideas.

4 Find out the movements the children like best and have another go at them. This time with help and encouragement from you to improve the quality of movement.

Further Steps

Ask the children to put any of the movements into a short sequence, or into a context, e.g. if you had leaping, hopping and running, **or** rowing, archery and riding, put them into the context of the Olympic Games.

Instant Rhymes

Age range: 6+
Time: 10 minutes
Aim: Recognising words of similar sound

On the blackboard write three words and, together with the children, find words which rhyme e.g.

bed	ball	bat
head	hall	cat
red	call	sat
said	small	rat
dead	shawl	gnat
bread	fall	fat
shed	stall	hat

1 Sit the children in a circle and establish the pattern: 'I want a rhyme in double-quick time, and the rhyme I want is bed.'

2 The children call out in turn: head, red, said, dead, etc. and the game goes on until no one can think of another rhyming word.

3 Choose someone to start the pattern with another word.

4 It can be developed by having more than one syllable or it can be competitive – pluses for correct rhymes, minuses or forfeits for false ones. You can be referee yourself in deciding who is first to call, or you can use a child.

Further Steps

A To get the idea that a rhyme is not necessarily consistent with spelling, you might write a list at random with words which can be paired; 'soundalikes' but not 'lookalikes' e.g.
bow bough; ruff rough; close clothes; climb mime; said red; flour flower.

B Introduce the idea of rhyming slang and then get the children to invent some, e.g.
crow and rook = book, women and men = pen, stomach and chest = pest.

MARINO INSTITUTE OF EDUCATION

ECHOES

Age range: 6+

Time: 15–20 minutes

Aim: To assist concentration and promote listening

Choose a venue or location which the children are likely to be familiar with e.g. the shopping precinct, the kitchen or <u>the main street</u> and list ten or a dozen words related to it:

traffic lights	parked car
crossing	sweet shop
litter basket	paper shop
prams	bus shelter
traffic warden	wooden seat
pavement	buskers

1 Explain you are to tell the children a story, and they will be part of it. Now allocate the words or phrases to small groups so that everyone is involved. They become traffic lights, buskers, etc.

2 Tell the children that whenever they hear their word or phrase they must echo it.

3 Now tell the story. Use it as a basis and play around with the possibilities. Try using various devices to catch them out, such as instant repetition of a word or phrase.

Further Steps

A Let the children choose the venue and the details.

B Let them tell their story.

Help here by saying that the story might include:

What you see, hear, smell.
How you behave.
How you feel.
What opinions you have (for instance about motorists who ignore your red light).

14

'STOP!' said the traffic lights. 'You can't cross my crossing whenever you feel like it. My crossing is a very important crossing. Just you wait there, on the pavement, until I say GO!'

The traffic warden was busy asking the driver of the parked car to move on. 'You're right beside the bus shelter,' he said, 'and that will never do. Parked cars and bus shelters don't agree.'

Down near the sweet shop the buskers were performing. Even the babies in their prams were laughing at their antics. For buskers, as everyone knows, can sing and dance and act and turn somersaults. But the old man coming from the paper shop wasn't laughing. Where was the wooden seat he sat on each morning to read his paper? Ah! there it was. The buskers were balancing it on their heads. Disgraceful!

The litter basket was very busy, what with sweet wrappings from the sweet shop, and litter from the paper shop. Does no one ever take pity on a poor little basket, and take the weight off it? Does no one think of emptying it? Not the babies in their prams (too young); not the buskers (too busy); not the traffic warden (not his job).

'My job,' said the traffic warden, 'is to keep the parked cars off the street.'

'And off me,' interrupted the pavement. 'Pavements are for people, not for parked cars.'

By this time the wooden seat was back outside the paper shop, the prams had moved on to the crossing, the traffic warden and the parked car had disappeared, and the buskers were dancing beside the bus shelter. But the traffic lights stayed right where they were, as traffic lights do, winking, 'My crossing, my crossing. STOP and GO!'

Sounds Like . . .

Age range: 6+

Time: 15–20 minutes

Aim: To use sounds as stimulus to vocabulary

NO LOUIS, THAT WAS <u>NOT</u> THE SOUND

See that you have the following articles at hand: pencil, coin, book.

1 Make a few sounds which children are asked to listen to with closed eyes, e.g.

tap of pencil along radiator
flick of finger on blackboard
scratch of coin on desktop
riffle of pages of a book

2 Then volunteers come out to try to repeat the sequence – usually with much vocal correction from the rest.

3 Don't say who was right or wrong. Go over the sequence with the pupils watching, giving the 'sound' words a good airing.

4 Using blackboard or card compile a list of verbs – tap, flick, scratch, scrape, hit, punch, slide and so on.

5 Add adjectives or adverbs – scratched lightly, a quick tap, and so on.

6 Ask for a volunteer to make a sound sequence.

HOMEWORK

Further Steps

A Invent your own words.

B Ask children to 'show' a word of their own – press, smooth, pat.

C Turn this into a game of guessing and taking turns to mime.

Now look here

The children can sit either at their desks or in a circle. These activities are built around close and careful observation.

A

1 This is a simple game which you can begin by demonstrating with a volunteer. You sit or kneel and look fixedly at an object in the room – a mark on the wall, a drawing pin in a picture and so on. By looking alternately into your eyes, your partner has to decide what you are staring at.

2 Degrees of difficulty can be built in:

   a) Say nothing if the guess is wrong.
      Just say yes or no.
      Give clues, such as 'getting warm', 'to the right', 'up a bit' and so on.

   b) By looking at something in broad terms – the clock.
      By looking at something in specific terms – the 2 in 12.

   c) Your partner can be allowed to go up, point and touch what is thought to be the object, or not.

3 Change over.

4 Ask groups to join up in fours or sixes to discuss how they got on.

B

1 This is a further game which you can begin by demonstrating with a volunteer. You sit or kneel and point at an object in the room – the keyhole in the door, the window catch and so on. By looking along your arm your partner has to decide what you are pointing at.

2 Degrees of difficulty can be built in:

   a) Just say yes or no.
      Nod or shake your head.
      Say nothing until the right answer comes.
      Give clues, such as 'You're almost there', 'Between there and the cupboard' and so on.

   b) By pointing at a whole object – a jug.
      By pointing at part of it – the handle.

   c) If there's space for moving around, your partner can point to, or touch, the object in question.

3 Change partners.

4 Have a class discussion about the event. Use the opportunity to increase accurate word usage.

NEWSPAPER TOWERS

Age range: 8+
Time: 10 minutes
Aim: To assist manipulative skills

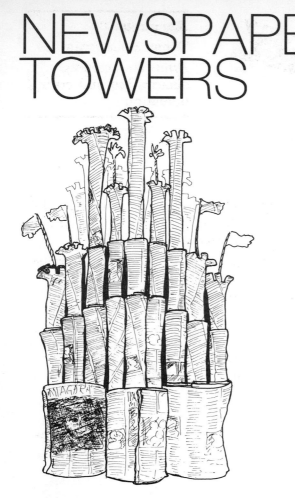

For this activity you will need a good supply of newspapers. Ensure that each pair has roughly the same amount of paper. This works well with any age. Ensure a reasonable space to work.

Further Steps

This activity also works well as a co-operative activity in small or large groups. Encourage as many different ways of building as possible.

1 Ask the children to work with a partner.
   Explain that when you say go, they have to build any structure they like, but it must be tall, and it must be stable. They can tear, twist, fold or crush the paper. They must not cut it. They must use all of it. Set them a time limit.

2 Start them off. Watch the efforts, but don't help.
   Warn them when their time is almost up. Stop them.

3 Let everyone inspect everyone else's work.

   Turn this activity into language use.

4 Pairs describe their structure.

5 Pairs answer questions about their structure.

6 Pairs are asked what proved difficult, and what successful.

MACHINERY

Age range: 8+

Time: 30 minutes

Aim: To encourage observation and co-operation

Starting with individuals, this activity develops into a huge machine which involves the whole class. First of all, explain the idea of a production line to the children. Then ask them to find their own space.

1 Tell the children that each of them is a machine which receives a piece of raw material from one side, processes it and then passes it on to another machine.

2 Encourage them to be inventive as to what they do with the 'raw material' – twisting, stamping with forehead, shaking, turning, squeezing, poking hole(s), etc. Their movements must be as robotic as possible.

3 Put them together in groups of 4 or 5, linking up their individual actions.

4 Now you can merge the smaller groups one by one until the entire class is working as one continuous process.

5 Start the class machine at a given signal so the process builds gradually. Increase and decrease the production speed.

6 Repeat the whole activity, this time adding appropriate sounds.

Games GAMES

Age range: 8+

Time: 15–45 minutes

Aim: Group enjoyment

Space for all games. Requirements for each game to be found within the explanation of that game.

Game One

Throw-a-face

Players sit in a circle. One player puts on a wide smile, wipes it off and throws it to another player. Player who catches it, changes it to a frown on his own face, throws it off and sends it to another player, and so on. Two sequences can be started at once, one person throwing smiles, the other throwing frowns.

Game Two

This is a hippopotamus

Players in circle, and any object (milk bottle, bean bag) is passed round. A passes it to B saying 'This is a hippopotamus.' B asks, 'A what?' as he returns it to A. A passes it back, and repeats 'A hippopotamus,' and so B passes it on to C saying 'This is a hippopotamus,' and so on round the circle, but always going back to A.

The word can be anything you choose, e.g. rhinoceros, lepidopterous, etc. So long as it's hard to say.

It seems at first to be a pointless game, but if done fast enough it's like a tongue-twister, and someone usually gets confused. You can leave this as a laugh, or knock people out till you find a winner.

Game Three

Pass

Players sit in a circle. One player passes (in mime) an imaginary object to his neighbour and so on round the circle. As he passes it he says 'It's made of . . . ' (jelly, lead, glue, feathers, air etc. etc.). The receiving player handles it accordingly until he passes it on saying 'It's made of . . . ' (poison, dynamite, super-glue, etc. etc.).

A variation which gives more scope is for the player to have to carry either across the circle or to 2, 3, 4 on his left or right.

Game Four

Sequence

Take a sequence such as, making a cup of tea, or starting the car, or washing your face. Stand in a circle. Player one begins the sequence with one simple single mimed action. The next player repeats the action and adds the next, and so on until the whole sequence is completed.

Game Five

Pass it on or Chinese whispers

This is the very simple game where a message is passed on in whispers. The end result is then compared with the original, usually to much hilarity!

WHISPER

DISLOCATED voices

Age range: 10+
Time: 15 minutes
Aim: To promote listening and language interaction

See that you have enough space to sit in a circle. Try this first with the whole group. Attempt it with smaller groups when they know the rules and are competent.

1 Explain to the children, now sitting in a circle, that when they are asked a question, the person on their right has to answer. Help them if they don't immediately all get it right.

2 Now you initiate any questions or conversation at all from the centre of the circle. Keep it lively. When everyone is sure of the game, you have a number of possibilities –

3 Vary the dislocated voice: 'Two to your right', 'One to your left', and so on.

4 People caught out take the centre and start a new conversation.

5 Eliminate those who get it wrong. Hesitation can be penalised. Keep it going in as lively a way as possible.

6 Eventually, when all are well versed, you can organise the whole class to get on with it themselves, preferably in 2 or 3 groups.

Can you, Do you, Will you listen?

Age range: 9+

Time: 25 minutes

Aim: To examine listening and the reverse

Ensure that enough space is available.

Here are four 'quickies' – exercises around the topic of listening, which can be done in isolation or as a warm up to a drama lesson, or separately, or in sequence.

The children work in pairs and preferably with the same partner throughout. With steps 5 and 6, swap their roles each time.

1 Tell the children they have to think of something they know a lot about, that they can easily talk about, e.g. my house, the way home from school, my pets, my favourite TV programme, my friends etc.

2 Tell them they have to keep talking, once started. Their partner must do the same. The point is that they are so busy talking that they don't listen.

3 Start them off, and after a minute or so, stop them.

4 Discuss with the children what happened.

5 Ask one partner to talk while the other constantly interrupts with questions, irrelevancies, 'helpful' comments and so on. See how easy or difficult it is.

6 Ask one to talk while the other one reacts with inattention, boredom, indifference, and so on.

7 In each case discuss the main features of the exercise.

8 What makes a good listener?

MORE SOUNDS

Age range: 6+

Time: 15–20 minutes

Aim: Practice in listening and creating sound sequences

This lesson explores sound – you will need pencil and ruler; comb and paper; chalk and blackboard.

1 Tell the children that you are all going to make sounds, and then find words that describe them.

2 Working with the whole class, try out the following ideas:

a) Sounds made by parts of yourself –

hands – clapping, rubbing
feet – drumming
fingers – flicking
lips – vibrating, puffing, popping
knees – knocking

b) Sounds made by your voice –

clucking
whistling
hissing
hooting
etc.

c) Sounds made by yourself and objects –

nails and desktop
palm and clothing
knuckles and desk
foot and floor

d) Sounds made by common objects –

pencil and ruler
comb and paper
paper itself
chalk and blackboard

3 Experiment with these, listen to them and talk about them. Find similarities and contrasts. Find words which define and describe them. Look for imaginative solutions, for example, when exploring the sounds made by a piece of paper pass the paper on to any child who can make a different sound from those preceding it. So you might get rustle, swish, crush, shake, and so on.

KNOCK
KNOCK
KNOCK

4 Split the class into small groups and ask the children to select some of the sounds to make up a sequence or story. They can devise the story, or you can suggest this one:

Old Jimmy blew on his hands to warm them. The frosty air made him cough and splutter. 'Home for me,' he thought, and shuffled off. Then he remembered. He'd meant to buy a paper. The shop bell pinged as he went in, and his coins chinked on the counter. He folded his paper carefully. 'Home to the fire, and a good read,' he said.

Further Steps

Fitting sounds to a poem. For example, *The Bird Table* lends itself to fun, both in speaking and in adding complementary sounds.

Here is one method of approach:

a) Read the poem to the class.

b) Ask for words that the children like the sound of.

c) Ask for words that seem to make a sound.

d) Ask the children to make the sound. (Remind them of the earlier possibilities.)

e) Put poem and sounds together. The simplest way is for you to read aloud while the children make the accompaniment.

The Bird Table

Ravens quarrel
Jackdaws swoop
Sparrows chat
Or loop the loop.

Starlings gossip
Blackbirds sing
On the clothes line
Magpies swing.

Chatter, chatter
Caw, caw
Hear the sounds
At my back door.

Chaffinch chirps
Near our back door
So many birds
Asking for more.

Splash goes the water
Scatter the seed
As they squabble over
Their winter feed.

Still and serene
The rock dove coos
As Lord of them all
He can pick and choose.

But Robin comes
When all have gone
And silence holds
Till he sings his song.

AB

Guess What?

Age range: 7+
Time: 20 minutes
Aim: To encourage mime skills and observation

Work with the class as a whole if in the classroom. If you want pairs at work you need more space. If possible, place around the classroom objects not usually found there.

WHAT **IS** MARIGOLD DRAWING?

Further Steps

A Mime a simple action, e.g. posting a letter, sawing wood.

B Discuss the kinds of movements made and make a word bank: slow, circular, jagged, smooth, and so on.

C Create a sequence of actions which are consecutive, or/and related, e.g. folding the letter → posting it.

1 Ask the class/pairs to look around the room, decide on any object they can see, and 'draw' it in the air in front of them. (If the children are working in pairs, they take turns 'drawing'.) Tell the children to draw slowly and to make a big picture.

2 Tell them to talk to their neighbours/partner about the object they 'drew', what shape it was, how big, where it was, why they chose it. Go round and monitor this. You can then discuss briefly one or two aspects of the work that you noticed or were interested in. Ask for volunteers to show what they 'drew'.

3 Now ask for volunteers to mime an object for the class to guess. (Ask the pairs to 'use' the imaginary object in some way together.)

4 Take turns as pupils guess.

Obedient Robot

BACK!

EXIT

Make sure you have a suitable space. Sit the class in a circle.

1 Choose someone to be the 'obedient robot' and someone to be the controller.

2 The controller orders the robot to do certain 'robotic' things – Turn right, turn left, stand, sit, stop, go, etc.

3 Simply call out 'Next please,' and the game goes on. The robot sits, the controller becomes the robot, and another controller is chosen.

4 You can develop it by asking for suggestions for additional instructions.

Further Steps

A 'Let's try something else' (e.g. sailor, dancer, farmer). Then go over with the class some of the orders you might give. Between turns, inject new ideas either of your own, or of the children's, or both.

B Have a disobedient robot.

C Art work based on the 'pictures' made by the performers.

D A short mime sequence. Work out a percussion signal for each of the foregoing characters. On each signal the children move as they think appropriate.

NOUGHTS & CROSSES

Age range: 7+

Time: 20–30 minutes

Aim: To enjoy a game which gives practice in spatial skills

A piece of chalk and a floor space – minimum 3 m × 3 m or 9 chairs safe to stand on. Mark off with chalk on the floor, or set out 9 chairs.

3 metres

3 metres

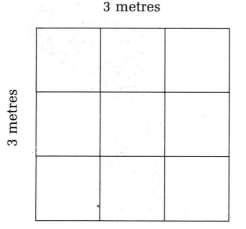

1 Arrange class in teams of 5 or 6. Ask each group to appoint a captain and give themselves a name.
Appoint a scorer and an umpire.

2 Discuss with children the game of noughts and crosses. (You will probably find some call it OXO, and some call it O's and X's.)

3 Tell them you are going to have a competition to find the champions of live noughts and crosses.

4 Write names on slips of paper and put them in a hat.

5 Draw them so that you get the order of play and who plays whom.

6 First pair of teams toss for first go, and to decide whether to be noughts or crosses.

7 Briefly explain that instead of marks on paper, they can use their team to fill the squares.

8 Establish how you might distinguish noughts from crosses.

9 Play off as a knockout tournament. It can be one game per pair, or the best of three depending on time.

Further Steps

Why not make this a playground game if it's a fine day?

Making up the Numbers

Age range: 7+

Time: 15 minutes

Aim: To encourage co-operation and number awareness

A reasonable amount of space is necessary for this activity as the children are physically creating numbers.

1 Select a number and ask the children to create it with their body shape. Try this with several numbers.

2 Put the children into pairs and try some more numbers. They will have to be more experimental, working together like this, using the floor, for example.

3 Combine pairs into groups of four. You can now give them larger numbers to work on.

4 Let the children select their own numbers and ask the rest of the class to identify the number.

Further Steps

A Use the floor exclusively, i.e. all numbers have to be read from above.

B You can repeat the whole activity with letters and simple words.

PHYSICALS

Pictures

Age range: 9+
Time: 20 minutes +
Aim: To assist body awareness

You need an open space in which pupils can work separately. Check they're dressed suitably for ease of movement.

1 Ask the children to find a space to stand.

   Explore the movements possible with parts of the body – trunk, head, arms, legs, shoulders, hands. Feed them suggestions as necessary.

2 Relax them. Tell them you are going to give them words which they can express with their bodies, standing or sitting or lying, etc., but not moving around. Use their knowledge of slow motion and give them a simple ritualistic countdown which they can use as they 'grow' into their chosen shape, to present a 'picture'.

3

happy	bored	angry
tired	strong	worried

Tell them the word. Ask them to think about it. Now move into it: '3 – 2 – 1 – freeze.'

4 You can now develop this in pairs. Using the same words ask the children to work their 'picture' out. You can then use the 3–2–1 procedure to grow into the shared image.

5 In turn, ask the pairs to illustrate a word. The rest of the class must try to identify the word.

PHYSICALS

The MODEL

This activity involves pairwork, with one partner 'modelling' the other into different positions. The passive partner lets him or herself be modelled into 'the picture'.

1 Put the children into pairs, A and B. Explain to them that you are going to give them the title of an activity which A will have to model B into. (A demonstration by the teacher will undoubtedly help.) At the end of each activity switch A and B.

2 Fishing
Playing the guitar
Pointing at the stars
Drinking
Combing hair
Sawing wood

Emphasise that there should be no speech. The model does not move itself, but stays in position when moved by the artist. Attention to detail is important, from all angles.

3 Combine the pairs to produce two models and two modellers. This time ask them to produce pictures involving the interactions of two people:

OH GOODY!

Shaking hands

Dentist and patient

Moving furniture

Roadworkers

4 Each time allow the modellers to go round to look at other ideas, before returning and switching roles.

Further Steps

A Use a story or poem the class are familiar with as a starting point.

B Build up three 'pictures' which form part of a sequence (before – during – after).

PHYSICALS

MIME SEQUENCES

Age range: 8+
Time: 15–20 minutes
Aim: Observation and attention to detail

Preferably an open space with a chair for each child.

1 Show a sequence of a simple kind, broken down into individual movements:

Pull up sleeves
Turn on tap
Pick up soap
Soap hands
Put down soap
Lather hands
Rinse under tap
Turn off tap
Dry hands
Pull down sleeves

2 Discuss this in all aspects –

What was I doing?
What was the first action?
What was the last action?
What was the simplest action?
What was the longest action?
And so on.

3 Ask the children to think of a simple sequence –

At home
At school
Sporting
Working
And so on.

Give help here. Avoid impossible or difficult things. Keep the sequences simple, functional and commonplace.

Write up a list of the choices, and then go through it in mime with the whole class, drawing attention to each significant action.

4 Organise groups of 4, 5, or 6. Tell them to sit in a circle. Tell them to number round.

Tell them to choose their sequence, and give a start number.

5 Groups now mime their chosen sequence consecutively round the circle. Help as required.

6 Groups choose a sequence to show the others who have to guess what is being mimed.

Further Steps

A Discussing as a peer group their result.

B Showing their result.

C Starting with a different choice, and a different number.

D Instead of merely adding an action, each subsequent mime starts from the beginning and recapitulates the action so far.

Freeze-frame!

Age range: 9+

Time: 45 minutes

Aim: To explore movement and co-ordination

This activity uses the technique of slow-motion to look at movement in sport. A reasonable space is necessary.

Further Steps

A Tennis – Doubles

Working together in fours can work very well. The participants need to be ready to cope with the variations of a rally!

B If you feel a large group, or indeed the whole class, can make it work, you can try to involve them all in a larger-scale football/netball game. Slow-motion is useful as a control factor.

1 Ask the children individually to work on the following sports activities:

throwing the javelin
scoring at netball
serving a tennis ball

In each case ask them to repeat it in very slow motion. At various points, at a given signal, you can 'freeze-frame' and then continue.

2 Let the children suggest further ideas.

3 Put them into pairs. Try now to develop co-ordination between partners, using the game idea of slow-motion and freeze-frame. Use these situations:

football – penalty-taker and goalkeeper
tennis – two partners
netball or basketball – two team-mates

It is very important that the children work carefully to establish a rapport with each other.

4 Let the children find their own ideas and share the results with the class.

MARINO INSTITUTE OF EDUCATION

The Games

You need a good space, and the children should be dressed suitably for ease of movement.

Agree on a control signal. Could be a handclap or a tambour.

1 Tell the pupils to mime any sport they like.

2 Narrow this down to specific sports and begin to comment on the quality of the movement. Feed in ideas. These can be based on aspects of the game itself, or aspects of the movement: slow/fast, stretch/confined, high/low and so on. In other words, aim for greater accuracy of recall and greater sensitivity of expression.

3 This could easily fill your time, but if you can go on, here are some ideas:

Further Steps

A Creating a short sporting sequence (a rally in badminton).

B Creating a sporting miscellany (Sports Day).

C Using commentary.

D Feeding in music, either to provide atmosphere or as something to 'work to'.

E Collecting pictures of sportsmen and women for classroom display or a class album, or following up any one sporting star over a season. This could be done individually, or by groups or as a class.

PHYSICALS

Taking a walk

PHYSICALS

Ensure that you have available a large space.

1 Sit your class down in the hall or any space where you can 'take your walk'.

2 Tell them a story. (See overleaf)

3 Briefly recap, especially those bits which you know you will use later. Try these out in movement. Encourage concentration, and 'getting into the part'.

4 'Let's do that story.' Tell the children that as you retell it, they can move to it.

   You cannot tell the story at the usual pace. You will need to watch the children's efforts, and see that they have time to do the movement sequences. To a large extent therefore they dictate the pace, but you must see that the onward action is not lost.

5 If you have sufficient time you could now read *The Bird* (or save this for another lesson).

Further Steps

A Art: Individual pictures of any one incident.

B Art: Individual aspects of the story combined to show the journey/gardening on a wall frieze.

C Devise another 'Taking a walk' story with the children's help.

PHYSICALS

Ann and Jimmy's Walk

'Mum! Why can't we go up the woods for a walk?' said Ann and Jimmy in chorus. They must have worked this out between them. 'You did promise.'

'I know, I must have been mad, when there's so much to be done. Come on then, no time like the present, and the sun's shining.'

So off they went, down the busy narrow pavement to the crossing, along to where the houses stopped and the fields began.

'There's no pavement,' said Mum, 'so keep in to the side and right behind. If anything comes, press yourself into the bank.' And that's what they did, and oh! the hedge was prickly if you pressed too hard against it.

'There's something tickling my neck,' shrieked Ann. 'Must be a creepy crawlie,' replied Jimmy.

But Mum said, 'Stop your nonsense Jimmy – it's you all the time. Look out, here comes a lorry.'

By this time they'd reached a gate. Mum climbed over, Jimmy slid underneath and Ann went through a hole in the middle. Then they peered through the gaps in the hedge at the traffic rushing past.

'Can't see me,' called Ann to a builder's van.

'Come on and keep to the path you two,' and so they did. It was Jimmy who decided that if you stretched on tiptoe you could see over the top of the waving corn.

'Just like a sea – all wavy,' said Ann, and it was Ann who knelt down and peered through the stalks.

'Just like a jungle,' said Jimmy.

'And just as full of creatures,' said Mum.

'Creepy crawlies.'

'Shut up, Jimmy,' said Ann.

Out of the cornfield they went, up a steep slope, across a ditch you could just jump, down the bank at the other side and then in front of them the woods, dark and mysterious and cool.

'Chases,' called Ann. 'Right,' said Jimmy, as he dodged off among the trees.

'Don't go far, and don't be long,' called Mum, but they'd already got too far away to hear. She settled down in the sunshine. 'I'll get a nice rest while I can,' she thought. And so she did.

36

The Bird

I could watch people working all day. Take Mr and Mrs Greenfingers. Very busy folk. Well she is. Always working. I watch them a lot. Quite often I go to sleep, I get so tired just watching them work.

I sit on my favourite branch, wings folded, eyes cocked, head to one side. I can see them but they can't see me. Even when I swoop down to catch a worm or a fly, I'm back on my perch before they know it.

Shh! That's them now. Take a peek with me through a chink in the leaves.

Trundle, trundle, trundle goes the barrow. Mr Greenfingers. He's stopped, lifts the tools out, one spade, one fork, one rake. He's bending down. No, wrong. He's sitting on the grass unlacing his boot. He's shaking some grit out. On it goes again. Lace it up. He stands. I know what he'll do now. Takes his hanky out, mops his brow. Takes his hat off. Mops his bald head. Puts it on again.

Look, here comes Mrs Greenfingers. Very bossy. She points, hands on hips. Oh poor man, he's got to carry her heavy water can. She's bigger than he is; she could carry it herself. Now she goes to the rose garden. Kneels down. From her pockets what does she take, scissors and string. Snip, snip, off with the dead heads. She ties the new branches in.

Oh dear! Now she's pricked her finger. If she knew I was watching she wouldn't suck it. Into her pockets she goes again. Takes out her gloves and puts them on. Snip, snip, snip, snip.

He's pulling up weeds now, and putting them in the barrow. He starts to dig. Holds his back, looks at the sky, digs again, holds his back, yawns. Sees his wife is looking. Digs faster.

She carries rubbish to the barrow. Dumps it. Picks up the rake. Rakes the rose garden.

Mr Greenfingers leans on his spade. Takes out his pipe. Sees his wife looking. Puts it away again. He goes to the barrow. Trundle, trundle, trundle round the corner.

His wife lifts the watering can and waters the roses.

What's that I see? A bird from next door, on the newly dug earth, stealing my worms.

Excuse me, I'll have to go. Time I chased him off.

Puppets– *a miscellany*

PHYSICALS

A

Here's a word or two about puppets.

1 You don't need elaborate ones, or elaborate theatres. You don't even need to get the children out of sight.

2 The subject matter is universal. The characters can be bad, good, foolish and so on.

3 The puppets can be:

The child's own painted hand
A paper bag quickly marked up
An old sock
A potato or turnip
An empty box
A sleeve puppet

Whichever type you choose, get the children to experiment with the possibilities of movement and voice. Encourage imagination!

i) *Hand or sleeve*

Each child has two (sleeves or hands) and can experiment with two characters:

an argument
a meeting

Try out different emotions – sad, happy, angry and so on.

Share the result.

B

Here are a few ideas developed from **A**.

Equipment: Junk and simple art materials.

ii) *From an old sock*

a) Paint on, stick on, or stitch on rudimentary features. (This is your art/craft work. Make it your language work as well.)

b) Recall with the children any story or stories they have done in class. Take an episode. For example, from *Red Riding Hood, Cinderella, Billy Goats Gruff.*

c) Ask the children to turn their puppet into any character they choose, and practise what it says and does.

d) Make up pairs. The pairs now have a possibility of two scenes to work on. Encourage co-operation in acting out.

e) Share work.

iii) *From an empty box*

a) Make a few puppets from boxes which will go over heads without damage to either. Tell children who they are: 'Foolish Jack', 'Mr Knowall', 'Contrary Mary'. Let the children try them on informally. *BE* the characters and so on.

b) Ask the class to tell you some of the things Foolish Jack gets up to, that Mr Knowall knows about, that Contrary Mary is awkward about, and list a few on the blackboard.

c) Make up pairs. Each pair is to choose and work out a sequence based on the list.

d) Invite pairs to run their sequence for the class. You might say, 'Who's ready to be Mr Knowall?' and of course Mr Knowall comes off the shelf and on to the volunteer's head.

iv) *From a paper bag*

a) Issue paper bags. Show children one or two ideas for faces for their puppet, e.g. a funny face, a fierce face, a sad face, and so on.

b) Children now make their own puppet face and 'try it on'.

c) Ask the children to find a partner. Tell them you will give them starters for conversations. You can work on the principle of the first one to speak starts, or you can designate 1 or 2 or A or B having first allowed them to decide which is which.

d) Here are some starters:

Well, and where have you been?

What makes you look so (miserable, sad, happy, etc.) today?

What's your favourite (colour, programme, game, food, etc.)?

Note:

Mostly these activities need nothing in the way of a theatre. Most provide opportunities for all the children concurrently. If you want more 'sophistication' then such rudimentary rigs as backs of chairs, a sheet draped over a rope, would suffice. A table turned on its side can be dangerous if the legs are not firmly weighted. A puppet theatre of course is fine, but unless it can be used for other activities you have to ask if it justifies time and expense in construction, and the space it takes up.

Helpers

Age range: 7+
Time: Up to an hour
Aim: To consider 'care'

Blackboard, chalk, and a space.

Class at the outset, pair work to follow, class to conclude.

1 Lead a class discussion on people who care for us, list on blackboard as agreement is reached, e.g.

Doctor	Father
Nurse	Farmer
Mother	Air/sea rescue

Further Steps

A Tell or read the story of 'The Good Samaritan'.

B Discuss the story in terms of the earlier work.

C Ask class to make pairs again, and work on any part of the story which shows caring.

2 Ask class to form pairs, and work out a short mime or role-play to show an example of caring. One of the pair must be taken from the agreed list. Help as necessary.

3 Ask pairs to tell you what their sequence was, or ask pairs to share their ideas.
OR
Ask some to show while others describe what interested them, what guided their choice and so on.

STORIES

The Tunnel Folk

Age range: 8+

Time: 40 minutes

Aim: To interpret a story in movement terms

Ensure you have an open space. Have stacking chairs arranged for the story-telling. Blackboard or labels and blu-tack.

1 Read the story.

Revise it, consolidate the children's understanding of it; and sharpen up their memory of it, in particular draw from them the images of movement, in particular those of the tunnel folk. Try to build up, from the children's responses, how they move; what rituals they might have; how they greet each other.

2 Ask children to form groups of three or four or five, to take a chair each with them to their own space on the floor. While this is being done, write up on blackboard, or pin up labels:

'We have our store against winter.'
'What games they play – marvellous games –'
'Sometimes the old and many-whiskered ones put them out.'
'They make friends up there.'

3 Tell the groups, as a whole, to try out the first one, and help them with ideas as they make their store.

Now tell them they can choose from the other three. This time go round the groups and help as necessary, with movement ideas, and the use of chairs improvised.

Further Steps

A Show work to the rest of the class.

B 'Such tales they tell of life up there within the great expanse of sky.' Ask groups to make their group story, and be prepared to tell it to the rest of the class.

Come with me, and I will show you my Kingdom. Tread softly lest you disturb my kin, the tunnel folk. Come down below the grasses which hide us. Take one last look at the sky broken into wild patterns by the wind-tossed flowers. This is my home, down, deep down in the cool gloom.

Cool and cavernous and dark is my home, but safe. Dark and safe and silent. Yet sometimes we tremble. We hear the sounds of many voices above us. Could they be the hunters calling, their dogs baying? Sometimes our roof of earth and roots shakes to their heavy feet, and the pressure of great wheels. Then we draw together. We cower till the danger is past. Who knows what might become of us if our tunnels are stopped by earth fall!

And such tunnels smoothed out and shaped by busy paws – a myriad web, a giant maze, a labyrinth too confusing for anyone but ourselves, the tunnel folk. We have our own homes down here – family homes. We have our store against winter. What else we have you must guess.

Our young ones, just as you, learn to know exactly where they are in our underworld village. What games they play – marvellous games of hide and seek, blind buff, tunnel tig. Sometimes the old and many-whiskered ones put them out. Then they have to invent games to play – don't ask me what – in among the tall grass zoo.

They make friends of course, up there, but they have to watch for the enemies who pounce and swoop, the clawed and furred and feathered ones. And when they come down here again, such tales they tell of life up there within the great expanse of sky. We sit in our meeting place and listen and laugh for we know that what they tell us can't be true but only imagination.

Now, if you'll care to watch your head, you can follow me down, and we'll explore . . .

RHYMES & SAYINGS

It is said that children don't have traditional rhymes and sayings any more. But watching and listening to their games reveals an often amazing wealth. Iona and Peter Opie's book – <u>The Lore and Language of Schoolchildren</u> – will provide good illustrations.

1 Ask if anyone has a rhyme or saying they use for a game. You might get a counting out rhyme, or a skipping rhyme.

2 If so, have some demonstrations.

TELL TALE TIT
YOUR TONGUE SHALL BE SLIT
AND ALL THE LITTLE DOGS
SHALL HAVE A LITTLE BIT...

Further Steps

A Find out the rhymes other members of your family remember.

B Research rhymes and make a book of rhymes.

C Invent a rhyme for the class to learn.

D Find a book which contains rhymes and games.

3 The foregoing should lead to a free-ranging conversation. This might include why people have rhymes, did they always have them, have other cultures got rhymes of their own, where would you look to find more, and so on. You might have one or two from your childhood, or you could read out the ones here. Do the children know them or a variation of them?

4 Try acting out a rhyme, or rhymes.

STORIES

Ask no questions
And you'll be told no lies
Shut your mouth
And you'll catch no flies.   BUSYBODY

See my finger
See my thumb
See my fist
— You'd better run.   THREAT

Ring a ring a pinkie
Ring a ring a bell
If ye brak the bargain
Ye'll go to hell.   A BARGAIN

What's for dinner, what's for dinner?
Irish stew, Irish stew
Sloppy semolina, sloppy semolina
No thank you, no thank you.   IRREVERENCE

God made the French
God made the Dutch
Whoever made you
Never made much.   JEER OR TORMENT

Tell tale tit
Your tongue shall be slit
And all the dogs in town
Shall have a little bit   SNEAKS

NURSERY RHYME TIME

Age range: 8+

Time: 25 minutes

Aim: To give practice in first person story telling

This activity can be enormous fun, besides giving good opportunities for story-telling. The idea is to extract a character from a familiar nursery rhyme and tell the story from their point of view. Additional details can be added, but the storyteller must stick to the original for the basic facts.

Further Steps

A If you want to expand this you could take the characters and invent other episodes in their lives. (The Secret Life of . . .)

B These episodes could be presented by groups, using rhymes which have more than one character, e.g. *Three Blind Mice, Jack and Jill* or maybe involving characters from other nursery rhymes.

1 Remind the class of nursery rhymes they are familiar with. This may be a good chance to talk about why they survive from generation to generation.

2 Explain that they will need to use the nursery rhymes to build up stories; give an example:

'I don't know where to begin. You see I was up on this wall, just sitting. I must have had a fright because the next thing I knew I was lying all of a heap on the ground. I was shattered.

'I think I must have passed out because I dreamt that the King came with all his horsemen and tried to fix me up. Then I heard one of them say, "It's a waste of time. He's had it!"'

3 Let the children share the stories in pairs and then in groups. Let the rest of the group try to identify the original figure.

True or False?

Age range: 9+

Time: 5–15 minutes

Aim: To give practice in relating anecdotes

Here's a game to fill an odd few minutes. There's no need to turn it into a saga.

1 Ask the pupils either to tell a true story or to make one up. Keep them simple and personal. The trick is not to give anything away with the tone of your voice or your facial expression. Here's one:

I was down town last night, and an old lady stepped off the pavement when the lights were red. She was knocked down by a car. The driver was in tears. But the old lady wasn't hurt much, the ambulance man said.

True or false? Try some more:

When I was five, I tried to ride my tricycle down some steps and knocked my front teeth out.

On my way to school I saw a man carrying a live chicken. He said it had escaped from a farm.

2 Keep them as short as that and even in five minutes you'll get through a few.

47

TREASURE!

Age range: 9+

Time: 45 minutes +

Aim: To solve a
problem

**Items of furniture usually found
in and around a school hall.
Photocopy and display the map
prominently (or distribute copies).
Set out the hall floor with
furniture, notices and chalk
marks to represent the terrain to
be covered.**

1 Bring the children round you.

Refer to the map. State the
object, which is to reach the
treasure, without losing a
member of the team through
accident or unnecessary risk.
Explain that the hall is laid out
like the map and answer any
questions asking for
explanations of the map.
Emphasise the problem of the
searchlights, which will flash
every 10 seconds.

2 Tell the children to make up
their own teams of any size
from 3 to 6, and then find a
practice space.

The teams must sit down and
discuss their plan of action.
They have to decide the best
route to avoid the hazards.

3 Tell the teams to practise in
their space any movements they
may find necessary when they
attempt to reach the treasure,
e.g. helping each other across
the river
leading each other through the
marsh

4 Sit the class down and remind
them of the geography of the
ground to be covered as set out
in the hall. Each team then in
turn has to attempt to reach the
treasure and return.

5 Discuss pros and cons of the
solutions, after each attempt.

Further Steps

Simplify the course: take
away searchlights, widen gaps
in fence.

Tell each team to memorise
their route and then each one
in turn has to try to negotiate
the course with their eyes
closed (or use blindfolds)
without touching the
obstacles.

STORIES

A – Open ground

B – Searchlights every 10 seconds

C – Rising ground

D – Electric Fence

E – Wildwood

F – The Cliff

G – Unknown Territory

H – Marsh

J – The rushing river

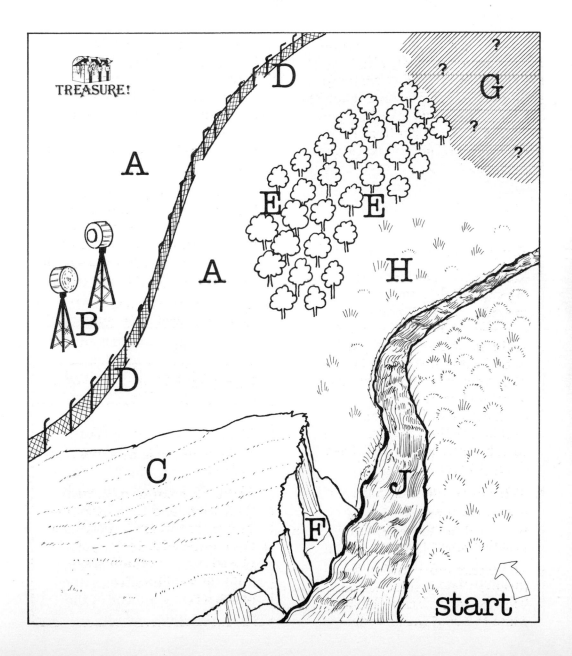

STORIES

The Boy Who Cried Wolf

Age range: 9+

Time: 30–45 minutes

Aim: To come in contact with a moral tale

See that you know the story, and have space to work in.

1 Tell the story in your own words.

2 Ask the children to imagine early morning, in the shepherd's kitchen. The family is there, and the boy is reluctant to go out on his own to mind the sheep.

   Ask the children to form family groups of 4 or 5. Each family to have a father, a mother, the boy, and other(s).

   Tell them you will come and ask a few questions about their family in a few minutes. Indicate the kinds of things they might decide – names, ages, responsibilities, etc.

   Ask them to create a family scene which begins a few minutes before the boy leaves for his first spell alone on the hills looking after the sheep. End the scene when he sets off.

3 Discuss the improvisations and any issues of interest arising from them, then discuss the issues as they appear in the story you told.

Further Steps

A *Alternative 1* Shows the boy still alive. Create a scene within the family showing what happened when they got him home.

B *Alternative 2* Shows the boy killed. What do you think the family said about it?

   Choose someone to be a local newspaper reporter, or someone from television to interview the families about it.

The Story

Once upon a time a boy was sent out to mind his family's sheep. It was lonely out there on the bare hillside and he got very bored. After a while he shouted, 'Help, help, the wolves are after me!' So his father and the other villagers rushed up only to find it was a hoax. 'Another trick like that,' said one, 'and if the wolves don't get you, we will.' And off they went.

Some time later much the same thing happened.

'Help, help, the wolves are coming!'

So up the villagers went only to find they had been tricked again. How angry they were. This time there were harsh words, threats and cuffs before they went back to their homes. But to no avail. The shepherd's boy shouted, 'Help, help!' a third time. Nobody came, and that was a great pity because this time the boy really was in danger. Later on when he didn't return home, the villagers set out to search. On the hill, where they had left him in anger, they found —

| Alternative 1 |

the shepherd boy, cold, frightened and bloody with claw and bite marks on arms and legs.

| Alternative 2 |

lying back against a stone, staring at the sky, the shepherd boy, who would never again call to anyone. His voice was silenced for ever.

Making Pictures

Age range: 8+
Time: 45 minutes
Aim: To compose living pictures

The classroom will do, but an open space is better if you want the pictures composed free of desks, chairs and so on.

2 List the ideas. Then say, 'Make a group any size up to and including five and find a free space to work in.'

3 Now ask them to make a picture from any one of the chosen activities. When complete, comment on the results and ask them to try another one from the list.

4 Make a series of pictures arising from the first one, to tell a story.

5 Try a picture of your own choosing.

6 Bring your picture to life (in mime only or as drama).

Further Steps

A Use a 'photographer' to arrange the group.

B Produce a sequence of before/during/after.

C Take an event which calls for pictures, e.g. a wedding or a birthday party.

1 What you're trying to do is to get the children to form group pictures (or tableaux). First talk about the children's activities – the sort of things they do and where they do them, e.g. skipping in the playground, at the swing park.

CHARADES

Age range: 6+
Time: 30 minutes
Aim: To have fun

It may be necessary to spend some time explaining the game and trying out a few appropriate words. On the other hand many of your children will know the television game 'Give us a clue'. If so, you can work on from that standpoint.

1 To play, divide everybody into teams of three or four and send one team out of the room to think of the word they are going to turn into a charade. You may find a group is quickly able to suggest words. If not, give them a word to start them off. Words with two or three syllables are best and the idea is that the team must act out each part of the word separately and then the whole word together, while the other teams watch. When the charade has been performed, the teams watching have to guess what the word was. If they get it right they score a point.

2 Teams take it in turn to leave the room and think of the words to act out.

3 Some good words for charades are: carpet (*car* and *pet*), cabbage (*cab* and *age*), kidnap (*kid* and *nap*), nobody (*no* and *body*), bargain (*bar* and *gain*), earwig (*ear* and *wig*), buttercup (*butter* and *cup*), snowdrop (*snow* and *drop*), football (*foot* and *ball*), mushroom (*mush* and *room*), marigold (*marry* and *gold*), understand (*under* and *stand*) and fortune (*four* and *tune*).

4 Remind the children that if they are going to present a word with two syllables they will need to act out three scenes. The first will show the first syllable, the second the next syllable and the third the word as a whole.

5 Charades should be mimed in absolute silence but you can make it easier by allowing certain words/sounds.

6 You can make it competitive by having scores, but the fun is the thing.

OUR TOWN

Age range: 7+
Time: 15 minutes +
Aim: To build up knowledge of the locality

Play this initially as a game.

1 Tell the children you are going to think of a destination and then give directions on how to get there. Explain that all directions start from the school gates.

The children have to guess where it is you want to go. The one who guesses right is next to play.

2 Help with precision of language where directions are ambiguous.

Further Steps

A The pupils have to say, 'This is how I got here this morning,' having picked a part of the town as their start point.

The class have to guess the start point. The one who guesses right is next to play.

B Help by introducing terms of time, of distance, of left and right, of key features, and so on.

C Pupils draw a detailed map of any local route they like. Encourage this, as map work, with symbols, a legend and clear printing.

D Pupils write a brief description of a building or place. Make a collage of all the efforts.

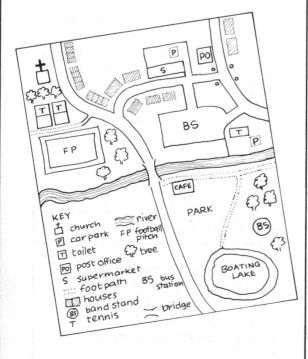

KEY
⛪ church   ～～ river
P car park   FP football pitch
T toilet   🌳 tree
PO post office
S supermarket
···· footpath   BS bus station
houses
BS band stand
T tennis   bridge

WHO AM I?

Age range: 9+

Time: 20 minutes

Aim: To improve logical thinking

This is a game of reaching an answer by logical thinking rather than guessing. So anyone who hazards a guess and gets the wrong answer needs to be encouraged to think carefully. You may have to limit the field of choice in order to ensure everyone can take part. For example:

Someone from sport.

Someone from entertainment: TV, music, films.

Someone in school.

1 Ask one pupil to pick a famous person, living or dead. He or she has to keep giving items of information, when questioned, until someone identifies the character.

2 If you want it as just fun, leave it at that. Next one to give details is the one who guessed.

3 If you want it competitive as well you can have teams. Scoring is on the basis of failure or success in identification, number of questions needed to make identification and so on. Guessing can be penalised.

4 Encourage the use of significant detail and discuss, where relevant, 'give-away' remarks.

Further Steps

To improve questioning techniques, instead of giving away details, only permit the answers YES and NO to be given to the questioners.

QUESTIONS & ANSWERS

Nursery rhyme time again

Age range: 9+

Time: 30 minutes +

Aim: To give practice in interviewing

This activity takes simple nursery rhyme characters and puts them into a TV interview situation. The interviewers may need paper and pencil to plan their questions; these questions are the key to what ensues.

1 Split your class into pairs or groups, remembering that in some cases you will have two or more characters to be interviewed together (e.g. Simple Simon and the Pieman). You will need an anchorman or presenter. This could be yourself.

2 Make a list with the children of well-known nursery rhyme characters e.g.

Georgie Porgie   Jack and Jill
Old King Cole   Miss Muffet
Humpty Dumpty Bo Peep
Simple Simon   Jack Horner

3 Explain what is to happen. Demonstrate the activity (taking both roles in turn) e.g. Jack Horner and TV interviewer.

4 Start off by everyone covering the same story. You can let them diversify later.

   a) Help interviewers to agree on the questions they will ask.

   b) Help the characters to decide what they might be asked and what they will say.

   c) Matching interviewers to nursery characters can be done by picking slips out of a hat.

5 Give time for rehearsal of interviews. Help as necessary.

6 Have a run through with everyone going at once.

7 Share one or two interviews with the whole class.

8 Then – let them choose their own story, prepare it, and share the interview with the class, in sequence.

As a starter, photocopy and distribute asking children to fill in the captions.

Further Steps

A Devise a whole programme using the characters in various ways — make up sequence, titles etc. Perhaps it could be a Breakfast TV programme.

B Try it on another class.

Recollections

Age range: 10+

Time: 30 minutes

Aim: To supply imaginary detail/make an imaginative response to an ambiguous tale

1 Read or tell the story. First, however, explain that children are to work in pairs. Explain also that after the story has been told, they must decide who is involved, why they are involved and what happened next.

2 Remind the children that the story leaves a lot of things unexplained. It's their job to explain their ideas to the class and of course to say what reasons lie behind them.

Point the children towards the things they should seek to discover, and then help pairs as required.

3 This is a 'telling' session which should lead to worthwhile contrasts and comparisons between different versions of the story. It's likely that there will be a demand to know what the story *really was*. In which case you, the teacher, might say 'Well, what *I* had in mind was . . . '

Further Steps

A List the people in the story, e.g. evil men, mother, hired hands, foreman, also anyone who might in some way be involved, and either give their view of the situation, or write it.

B Act out what happened to the foreman.

Recollections

It stays with me, that memory of my mother's grief, when many another thing has faded.

Those were evil days and evil men; about their secret business. You could hear them if you'd a mind to. Late at night in the stillness of the mountains they would move stealthily with their deadly load across to the West.

The ponies were as silent as their masters and as sure-footed. Faint on the night air I would hear their muzzled breath, almost feel the careful placing of hoof on treacherous rock.

Those were the times of trouble. I was young and foolish then. Not for me the staying indoors, or heeding my mother's urgent warnings.

'Decent folks stay behind closed doors when the darkness comes,' she would say. Little she knew that I would creep from my bed, and stand on top of the wagon lying behind the sheds, for all the world like a sentry. I would imagine the passes thronging with men and animals, about a deadly purpose.

A mixture of fear and thrilling excitement was in me then, fed by the fireside tales of the hired hands.

'Keep out of it, and you'll not be harmed,' they would say. But I knew in my heart that one night, some night, the hoofs would stop, the footsteps would reach our door, rough voices would speak, and in the morning, when such things would seem to have been dreams, there would be one fewer at the breakfast table.

And so it was. I was asleep that dreadful night, and heard nothing. In the morning I found my mother weeping and our foreman gone.

I never went out to the wagon again.

POSSESSIONS

Age range: 9+

Time: 45 minutes

Aim: To exercise reasoning

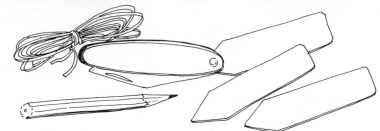

Have the grid duplicated or up on the blackboard.

See that children have pen and paper. Prepare the 'lost' jacket with suitable contents. Try to be as enigmatic as possible.

1 Tell the children that these sets of objects were found in people's pockets. Ask them who they think had the first set.

Now ask them to go ahead and write down as many of the other people as possible in the time. Tell them not to worry about the order. Stop them and ask what the results were, how they justify them, whether there were any alternative answers, and so on.

2 In turn, ask children to make up a list of 3 objects for a person of their choice. Then they ask the rest of the class, 'Who am I thinking of?'

3 Now show the children a jacket which has been found. Go through the pockets, display the contents, talk about them and leave them on show.

4 Ask children to work with a neighbour. Tell them to work out who the owner was or is, and be ready to make a report to the class in as much detail as possible.

5 Help pairs with this. If desirable put an outline on the blackboard for the reports to build on.

6 Ask for reports, and discuss with the class strengths and weaknesses of conclusions reached in terms of the evidence offered.

Further Steps

Create an episode in the person's life, either:

by writing

or by acting out.

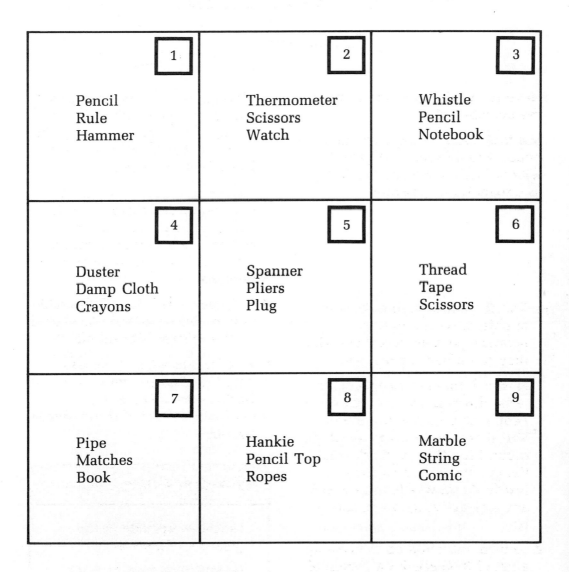

1		
Pencil Rule Hammer	Thermometer Scissors Watch	Whistle Pencil Notebook
Duster Damp Cloth Crayons	Spanner Pliers Plug	Thread Tape Scissors
Pipe Matches Book	Hankie Pencil Top Ropes	Marble String Comic

QUESTIONS & ANSWERS

Detection

**Photocopy and distribute the layout and clues.
Lay out relevant objects for inspection on a table.**

1 When the police were called to the house by a distressed householder, this is what they found:

   a) A front door off its hinges.
   b) Smashed, ransacked bedroom and lounge.
   c) Items missing: pictures, jewellery, VCR and computer.
   d) An iron bar lying near the gateway.
   e) Tyre marks under the window.
   f) A small balaclava helmet on the front path.
   g) A bloodstain on the window sill.
   h) A large pair of gloves lying on the hearth.

2 Arrange your children in groups of 3 or so. They will need pencil and paper for rough notes.

3 Go over the evidence briefly with teams. Tell them they are to imagine they are the police who were called in. Their task is to consider carefully all the evidence and to work out exactly what happened.

4 Go round and help with this.

5 Give the class, as a whole, some help in shaping up their reports, and give them time to organise themselves so that each one in every group is involved in presenting it.

6 Each group has to tell the rest of the class their version of the sequence of events. You can chair and handle any discussion.

Further Step

Organise groups to make written reports.

🛡️ POLICE REPORT

NAME

ADDRESS

CRIME COMMITTED   DATE

CLUES

WRITE CONCLUSION OVERLEAF

SKETCH PLAN OF BUNGALOW

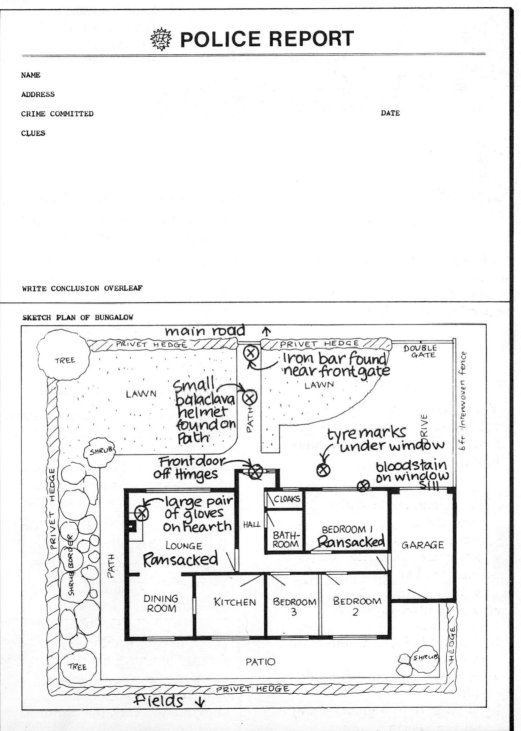

main road ↑

PRIVET HEDGE

DOUBLE GATE

TREE

LAWN

⊗ Iron bar found near front gate

LAWN

Small balaclava helmet found on path ⊗

6 ft interwoven fence

SHRUB

tyre marks under window ⊗

DRIVE

PRIVET HEDGE

Front door off hinges ⊗

bloodstain on window sill ⊗

SHRUB BORDER

large pair of gloves on hearth ⊗

CLOAKS

⊗

HALL

BATH-ROOM

BEDROOM 1 Ransacked

GARAGE

PATH

LOUNGE Ransacked

DINING ROOM

KITCHEN

BEDROOM 3

BEDROOM 2

HEDGE

TREE

PATIO

SHRUB

PRIVET HEDGE

fields ↓

Dialogues

Age range: 7+

Time: 10 minutes +

Aim: To promote quick thinking and response

What you have here is a number of quick-fire unpremeditated conversations. Since they are not in role, the children could hardly be said to be role-playing, but what happens is just a step away and so your 'Further Steps' is more or less self-evident.

You need pairs for any of these. They all work in the same way and are not pre-arranged, so the responses must be on the basis of what is heard, but each individual, when speaking, has the chance of directing the course of the conversation.

1 Pairs then, and a free space. The classroom would do, but would be pretty noisy. Ask them to number 1 and 2, in their pair. Explain that you are going to give a starter word or phrase and then say 'Go one' or 'Go two' and that's the phrase to begin the conversation with. Agree on a control for stopping each conversation.

2 Any starter phrase will do, but it would be worthwhile thinking in terms first of a schematic approach, e.g. you might use as a basis:

accusation	'What have you done with it?'
advice	'I shouldn't touch that if I were you.'
direction	'Go over there and wait.'
help	'Can you give us a hand?'
sympathy	'I feel awful.'

3 Don't have postmortems or serious discussions. It's language flow and plenty of it, with involvement and enjoyment. Work the children hard and fast.

YOU'RE ONLY PRETENDING!

Further Steps

A Build in character or role.
B Build in action.
C Build in situation.

For example 'Go over there and wait.'

- Characters could be:

  Policeman to suspect.
  Nurse to patient.
  Parent to child.

- Action could be:

  Lead up to cross-examination.
  Prelude to an X-ray.
  Wait while I buy the tickets.

- Situation could be:

  Street snatch of handbag.
  Suspected cracked rib from P.E.
  Start of journey.

OPENINGS

WILD GREEN JUNGLE

Age range: 9+
Time: 1 hour
Aim: Imaginative reconstruction

Make sure you have, outdoors if possible, an ample space. If outdoors, you really do lie down and look in the grasses.

1 Ask —

'Have you ever put your face down in the grass – right down close to the ground – maybe on a hot summer's day? Peering round and through?

'Lie on your stomachs, cup your face in your hands, and look down, look round, look through. (Imagine) you are in a summer field of long dry grasses. What do you see? Don't tell me now.

'Now, when I stop talking, I want you to say, very quietly, what you can see. That's everyone. You can stop whenever you've run out of ideas, or when I stop you – whichever suits. Are you ready to start? Right, begin your commentary now.'

2 Invite anyone to tell you one thing they saw (imagined), e.g. centipedes, ants, moths, flies.

3 Invite the children to show the kind of movement their creatures made, and lead into a movement session which can become more controlled. One way of organising this would be to take, e.g. one part of the body to establish the kind of movement a caterpillar makes, another to establish a butterfly's movement and so on. Be specific and don't accept vague interpretations.

4 Having explored this, ask for sounds made by mouth or parts of the body, e.g. hands rubbing together.

5 Link up sound and movement.

6 Put the children into groups of 4 or 5. Ask them to create one of their creatures together – as a group effort.

Further Steps

A Repeat step 6, but let them develop an imaginary creature from another planet.

B Follow-up artwork — collage of space creatures.

OBJECTS OF INTEREST

Age range: 9+
Time: 1 hour
Aim: To produce an imaginative response

Any object or garment which seems to have some intrinsic interest – historical, personal or whatever, e.g.

A foreign coin
An old toy
A rusty key
A battered money box
A document
An ancient book
A top hat
An old-fashioned shoe or boot

1 Let children see, touch, smell, discuss the object or objects (a picture would do, but it is not so stimulating).

2 Promote free-ranging discussion.

3 Guide this into channels suggesting age, owner, use, contact.

4 Ask children to form small groups and find a working space.

5 Now say something like: 'Make up a short play in which we see the object used by the owner. You can mime the object in preparation but when you play to the class you can actually have it.

'You will have to decide who the owner was, and which of you will play that part, and who the others were.'

6 Set the groups to work. Encourage activity-related discussion, and help to resolve problems.

7 Stop everyone, and say something like: 'Show me the picture of how your play begins. When I clap my hands, run through. When you're finished, sit and watch those who haven't.'

Further Steps

A As an alternative to acting out, tell a story involving the same factors.

B Again, as an alternative, write a script based around the object.

Superstitions

Age range: Any age

Time: 30 minutes

Aim: To look at our own and other people's superstitions

MY LUCKY DAY...

SCHOOL

This is only meant initially as a brief introduction to superstitions. In all probability everyone will know about walking under ladders.

1 Tell the children about any superstition you're familiar with e.g. mentioning *Macbeth* in the theatre; throwing spilt salt over your shoulder.

2 Good luck and bad luck. Talk about what other people feel is bad luck and good luck (umbrellas put up indoors = bad luck, a black cat crossing your path = good luck).

3 Do age and education make a difference to people's belief in superstitions? Bring in old wives' tales, fortune-tellers, astrology.

4 'A bad day' – work on an improvisation which shows someone's 'Bad Day', in groups of 4 or 5.

Further Steps

A If it's near to Hallowe'en, apply thoughts to its derivation, meaning and ritual.

B Track down some local lore, if possible –

'Red sky at night is shepherd's delight,
Red sky in the morning, is shepherd's warning.'

'Step on a crack, you'll break your mother's back.'

'Bad luck to look at a new moon through glass.'

C Design album front with the title 'Good Luck, Bad Luck'.

A View of the Sea

Age range: 9+

Time: 1 hour

Aim: To respond imaginatively to the printed word

Percussion instruments are not essential but will extend the possibilities. If you have percussion instruments, set them out for the number of groups you decide upon. 5 or 6 children to a group should do. If you would like children to see passage, run off copies beforehand.

1 Read the passage and discuss it in general terms, leading towards an understanding of personification. (What was said by the pebbles? How did they feel?)

2 Ask the children to make a sound pattern of John's progress to the sea. Groups play back results to the class and discussion should be encouraged. The sound pattern need not rely entirely upon percussion. Vocal, non-verbal and other environmentally produced sounds can be employed. If your children are new to this kind of work they may need a number of examples of the qualities of the different percussion instruments.

3 Ask the children to show what John saw when he 'plunged into silence'. Ideas to base this on can be discussed either beforehand with the whole class, or with each group as they work. What is intended here is a short movement session based on the undersea world. Move around and help them in their groups.

4 The groups might show their movement ideas to the class, or, knowing the ideas coming from each group's preparation, you can base a movement session for the whole class upon them.

Further Steps

A Writing based on the undersea world.

B Make a collage called 'Seabed'.

John ran breathless to the sea. His legs swept the dune grasses, and sand scattered, punched up between his toes, and lay there patterned, footprinted, as if to say 'Me again?' The pebbles flung themselves about (if they were small), stayed firm if they were large, as if to say, 'Shift yourself!' There was a dead branch, sea-withered and white. John ran along it, balancing. The branch rocked and swayed a bit, as if to say, 'Get off my back!'

Then the water, waves which swelled and
    beat
    Undertow which caught the feet
    Sliding on unseen weed
    Into the moving deep
    Freed
    From the earth
    Plunging into silence.

Verse time

Age range: 10+
Time: 20–30 minutes
Aim: To open up a
poem's meaning

If you decide that the children should see the poem, run off enough copies beforehand.

1 Children read the poem silently.

2 Invite responses. The activity may change in the light of the responses. However, a possible plan is set out here:

3 Ask children for words or phrases they like. If so, why? These can be read out and evaluated.

Ask for words or phrases they would like explained. Get explanations from other children if possible.

Move discussion on to imagery. Why sporting terms? What have they to do with what the poem is about?

What is the poem about? What is it trying to say about the future? Who is saying what, and to whom?

Have the young a special duty for the future of the world?

What title would you give the poem?

We're here in the blocks, ready to run
Eagerly poised for the starter's gun
Pay attention
Here's a declaration
To folk of every nation
Station
Situation
We're ready for the gun
Ours is the future
We hold it in trust
We are its reapers
We shall join worlds
Make friends on the way
We are the future, the future, the future,
Tomorrow's our day.
Tomorrow, tomorrow, tomorrow.
We shall dare,
We shall care,
Treasure who's there
Running to the universe' end
Bang!
The gun —
We are off
We're running
We're coming, my friend.

Emma's Week

Age range: 10+
Time: 1–2 hours
Aim: To reconstruct episodes from history based upon a diary

Pencils and scrap paper.

Diary extracts either on blackboard or photocopied.

1 Explain that you have come across a number of pieces of writing from a long time ago. Ask the children to make groups of 3 or 4 and read through.

2 Tell the class that you would like them to –

   a) Fill in the gaps.
   b) Discover the sequence.
   c) Decide what the writing is (letter, story, diary etc.).

3 Get feedback on these points and get groups to support their conclusions.

   Ask the groups to get two kinds of information from the diary –

   a) What is told.
   b) What can be reasonably inferred.

   This should result in a picture being built up with Emma at its centre.

4 You now have enough information for one, or a number of the following activities which may be best done in groups or individually depending on your choice.

5 a) Write a description of Emma's household on party day.
   b) Write another week of her diary.
   c) Write the same week for John's diary.

Further Steps

A Work out all the people Emma related to:

Emma and mother
Emma and doctor
Emma and father
Emma and John
Emma and cook
Emma and governess

and develop a series of role-plays based on what was in the diary, and also on what might have happened.

B Script a short scene based on one of these role-plays.

C Find out something about a Victorian children's party, and write a description of what Emma's party might have been like.

Monday 6th

Today began with poultices and that horrid, horrid blackcurrant drink to cure my chest. Oh dear! How much easier to be strong and play like .... But girls don't do that, especially not rich girls.

Sunday   187

Rushed home in the carriage from church. Bed and a roaring .... , Dr Brown looking very serious. Papa says 'No party for you next weekend, invitations or no invitations, unless you've been out walking.' I'm so hot!!!

Friday 10th   1879

Cook very bad .... today. Kitchen very hot. 'Little girls should know better than to interrupt the work,' she says. Still, I did walk out today. With nannie. In the park. (There's a large .... cake in the pantry.) I hope Mama tells Papa. About the walk I mean.

.... 7th   1879

Two letters today. That makes 28 more to come. Nannie says I'm a lot better. Only one more day for poultices. How nice it would be to be allowed out of bed! J .... gets all the fun and never comes to visit me. Brothers!

Wednesday   Sep   79

Up today for a short time. Miss Henderson really is nice. She thinks of all sorts of things for me to do. ('You're a first-class water-colourist, Emma.') How much nicer though to be able to be playing outside on the lawn. I can hear John rushing about and sho.......ng as usual.

I haven't coughed once today, and it's nearly lunch time. Cook's a dear. She made me a *special invalid* meal.

Saturday 11th September 1879

I'm so tired!

Such a bustle of preparation! Such a noise of games! Such food! (John and his friends are greedy pigs) and oh dear! I'm so tired. I shall finish this to........................... .

Thursday 9th September 1879

The postman came in today with heaps of .... Please, please Papa don't stop the party now. Nearly everyone is coming. Even John's friends. Ugh!

THE NUMBERS GAME

Duplicate the table, or write it up on the board. Have pens and scrap paper handy.

EIGHT MORE LIVES TO GO BENSON.

1 Ask the children if they know of any saying or expression which contains a number.

Provide one if necessary.

2 Sit the children in pairs with pen and paper. Introduce and explain the table. All the children have to do is to write numbers down the right hand side to show which corresponds with which. Do one with them.

3 After a few minutes report results.

Further Steps

A Explain meanings as necessary.

B Put phrases into contexts e.g. 'Bill's leg has healed now and he says he's a hundred per cent fit.'

C Start a list which can be added to as examples are discovered.

What You Have To Do

Find out which explanation on the right hand side goes with the saying on the left hand side.

Just write the numbers 1–11 in the boxes down the right hand side as you solve the puzzle.

Start with the ones you can do.

1	Elevenses	Gabbling away	
2	He's one hundred per cent	A cat	
3	Putting two and two together	Thirteen	
4	A baker's dozen	A mid-morning drink	
5	Talking nineteen to the dozen	He's fit and well	
6	They're ten a penny	Reaching the right conclusion	
7	Six of one and half a dozen of the other	Really cheap	
8	It has nine lives	Someone's fist	
9	Cat o' nine tails	Take care of things in time	
10	A bunch of fives	A fearsome weapon	
11	A stitch in time saves nine	Both equally to blame	

Age range: 10+
Time: 1 hour
Aim: To experience a simulation

Duplicate the letter, or write it up on the blackboard. Art materials, pens, pencils and paper.

Further Steps

A Using the information developed so far, devise and act out a TV advert for the area.

B Work on Mr and Mrs Hamilton's reactions to the Tourist Board's letter and brochure.

C Imagine the holiday goes ahead as planned. Work on incidents from the Hamiltons' holiday and share them with the whole group.

1 Imagine you are working for the Tourist Board, and are responsible for promoting business in your small seaside fishing town. You receive the attached letter and so you decide to send straight away to the Hamiltons, in reply to their letter:

a) the holiday brochure encouraging people to holiday in the area
b) the hotel advertisement.

2 In groups of 4 or 5 ask the children to make a list of the facilities a hotel might need in order to cater for the needs of this family. Then, using the art materials to hand, ask them to:

a) design the front cover of the holiday brochure
b) design the advertisement for the hotel in question.

Each group could split its resources on the two tasks.

3 This can be shared and discussed at the end of the session. What are the needs of each age group? What assumptions have people made?

COPY

The Tourist Board
Little Bramlingham-by-Sea

Dear Sir or Madam,

Bramlingham-by-Sea has been recommended
to us as a good place for a family holiday.
There are seven of us altogether – myself, my
husband, our three children (9 months, 5 yrs
and 10 yrs) and my parents, who are retired
but very active.

Perhaps you could send us a brochure of
Bramlingham-by-Sea and also recommend a
hotel.

Yours sincerely,

Emma Hamilton (Mrs)

Rumour

Age range: 10
Time: 45/60 minutes
Aim: To consider rumour

1 Ask two good readers to read the script to the class. Give them time to look at it beforehand if possible. If you feel it beneficial, ask another pair to read it, simply to reinforce the knowledge of the text.

2 Talk about rumour and stories.

3 In pairs work out Jimmy's story, i.e. what actually happened.

4 Tell the children that Jimmy's story has gone the rounds a bit, and Harry has got hold of it. What story does Harry pass on to his pals? This is the story you want them to invent, and later tell the class.

Help pairs as necessary.

5 Volunteers tell Jimmy's story to the class. Other volunteers tell Harry's story to the class.

Further Steps

A In groups, role-play the meeting with Harry. Begin from, 'Wait till I get him!'

B Ask them to show you another situation where rumours can distort the truth.

C Discuss rumour in wartime.

Who Says?

a   Jimmy? He was killed right enough. Died after that accident.

b   Killed? Who told you?

a   Harry.

b   And who told him?

a   I didn't ask.

b   You should've.

a   Why?

b   Well, you know what Harry's like – anything for a story. If he doesn't get the wrong end of the stick he makes it up.

a   Still. Jimmy's dead. He wouldn't make that up.

b   The trouble is he gets to believe things after he's told a few folk. You should have asked him.

a   Poor old Jimmy.

b   Yes. And just from falling off his bike.

a   On his head, remember.

b   Wait a minute. He hit his shoulder.

a   Still – on a concrete pavement.

b   No. He was on the grass.

a   Who told you?

b   I don't know. I just heard.

a   So you could be just as wrong as me.

b   Or just as right. Come on.

a   Where are we going?

b   To Jimmy's place. Come on. His mum –

a   Wait a bit. Who's that over there?

b   It's Jimmy.

a   On his bike.

b   With a bandage on his knee.

a   Who's he with?

b   Harry.

a   Dead! Wait till I get him!

Survival

Age range: 11+
Time: 30 minutes
Aim: To solve a problem

Have pens and paper handy.

1 Form groups of about 3 children.

Provide each group with some scrap card and paper.

See that each group has at least one pencil or pen.

See that each group is sitting at a desk or table so that they can talk to each other.

2 List on the blackboard –

Sleeping bag, matches, compass, tent, groundsheet, map, meat, bread, tea, penknife, axe.

3 Now set the scene, and give the task.

You are going on a week's survival course in the hills. Part of the exercise is to see what you can do without. Of the eleven items you can only take eight. Which will you leave behind, and why?

4 Help as necessary and after a few minutes explain that you will want them to explain their decisions and justify them.

5 Reporting back session.

Further Steps

A Discuss expeditions, voyages and so on, of a tough kind where survival depends a great deal on good preparation.

B If there is one currently operating, follow it up and make a diary of events.

Publications

The classroom will do, but a bigger space would do better, provided there are tables and chairs and you won't disturb others with noise.

Large sheets of paper – coloured pencils or pens.

One or two cassette recorders.

1 Split the class into working groups of three or, at most, four.

Lead discussion on comics. Do they read them? What do they read? What is popular/ unpopular? What improvements would they like to see? (Layout, subject matter, illustrations, cost, frequency, etc.)

2 Give them their task. Suppose they were about to launch a new comic for their own age group; how would they advertise it? They are responsible for publicity. They have to prepare advertisements for any one of the following:

Television
Radio
Newspapers

Go over with them what might be included, what the style would be. Would they have a slogan, or a catchword, a character, or a logo? In other words, support them with plenty of ideas.

3 If they choose television, they will have to do a live performance.

If they choose radio, they will do either a live or a taped performance.

If newspaper, either a statement or a graphic with words. These would be displayed after being introduced to the class.

Further Steps

Collect advertisements for comics and magazines and look at the way they work.

DECISIONS

THE TIME BOX

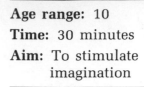

DECISIONS

Have pencils and scrap paper handy. Duplicate the newspaper report and the poem, or write it up if you think it will be more efficient than just reading it.

1 Read or show the following report, and then the poem.

   Discuss both, but especially the poem which needs 'opening up'. Establish what the writers of the poem intended with their chest and its contents, and also what they ask of us.

2 Organise groups of three or four, and give them their task.

   What would they choose to leave for a future finder? They are allowed ten items.

   Where would they hide the time box?

   What message would they include?

3 Bring the groups back together and discuss their ideas.

Further Steps

A A scrapbook of messages, with a title and illustrations.

B Ask them to go back to their groups.

   Could they prepare a short presentation to be videotaped showing what it's like to be 10 yrs old today? The video would be shown in 100 years' time. What would they demonstrate?

Cutting from the *Avondale News*

Workmen demolishing the Town Mill last week unearthed a heavy chest which was later opened by the curator of the local museum. The contents, when carefully cleaned, will be on show to the public. At present it is not known what they are but they are believed to date from 1887. However, we understand that the following verse was inscribed on the underside of the lid.

> To you, who find this chest, take care
> Within its hold are objects rare.
> Through many a year they've lain alone
> Beneath a floor of solid stone.
> Think you, who live in future days,
> Upon us now — our lives, our ways,
> Then leave yourselves, as your bequest
> What of your time you think the best
> That someone finding it may say,
> 'That's how they lived, in their own day.'

MOVING HOUSE

HILTON, I'VE FORGOTTEN THE BUDGIE!

You need pencils and scrap paper and tables.

1 Here's the situation:

The Shaws are moving to a place 200 miles away. Mr Shaw is busy. He's sitting in the car and thinking of all the things he has to do in the first few days after moving in, and this is how the conversation goes:

2 Mrs Shaw: 'What are you writing dear?'
 Mr Shaw: 'Just another little list – '
 Mrs Shaw: 'You'll get car sick!'
 Mr Shaw: 'And you'll have an accident if you don't watch where you're going.'
 Mrs Shaw: 'Lists!'
 Mr Shaw: 'You'd be in a fine old state if someone didn't do the organising and planning. Now you stick to your driving and I'll sort out my thoughts. There certainly won't be time to think when I'm trying to organise the removal men . . . '

3 Make groups of 3 or 4 and ask them:

What will be on Mr Shaw's list when they reach their new house? Your job is to make up the list. Just get someone to write while you all contribute ideas.

4 Help as needed and after a few minutes stop them at the end of the item they are writing. Hear one or two lists.

5 Ask them to be very critical and go through their list. Turn it into a list of things which must be done and the order you think they should be done in. (Introduce the concept of priorities.)

DECISIONS

Further Steps

A Have a formal reporting session. Groups form a panel which explains and justifies the list and handles questions and/or discussion.

B Put the lists on to large sheets and display them for everyone to 'go walkabout' and discuss them informally.

C Pick out items which need to be made more detailed e.g. being admitted to the new school, meeting the next-door neighbour, telephoning the doctor, getting the gas supply connected.

D Role-play a chosen situation in the existing groups.

E Role-play an incident where something went wrong, and show what your solution was.

THE KEY!

List

Don't forget the Rabbit!
New address.
Key.
Milkman.
Turn on water.
Gas and Electric.
Telephone.
New School.
Health cards – Doctor.
Meet neighbours.
Change disc on dog's collar.
Connect freezer!
Nearest Church.
Shops – order paper.
Clubs – Tennis, Golf, Slimming.
Street map.
Kettle – cup of tea!

Neighbourhood Matters

Age range: 10+

Time: 1 hour +

Aim: To help create social awareness

Tables, chairs, paper, pencils. Duplicate map, or draw it on the blackboard.

A rich man has left money for a 'fine new building' in his will. It has to serve 'all the people of the town, and it can, if necessary, replace an existing building'. He wants the children of the town to be involved in choosing what the building is to be, and helping to plan it, because he says in his will: 'They are the citizens of the future'.

No idea will necessarily be carried out exactly as suggested, but his executors have asked the Town Planners to judge entries from local schools. The winning entry will then be implemented.

1 The Town Planners have drawn up the following guidelines:

Write briefly what you feel the building should be.

Say why this is your choice.

Say whether it is to replace an existing building and, if so, why.

Say who will benefit most from it.

Where in your town would you want it built?

Why have you chosen that particular site?

With a sketch, and explanation, indicate what the building would look like.

2 Go over this carefully with the pupils. Write up significant information. Do this as a class. Now ask them to form working groups, no less than three, no more than five, arrange themselves around a table, provide themselves with scrap paper and pencils, and set to work.

Help as needed.

3 Stop them at a given point, and ask them to tidy up their planning so far.

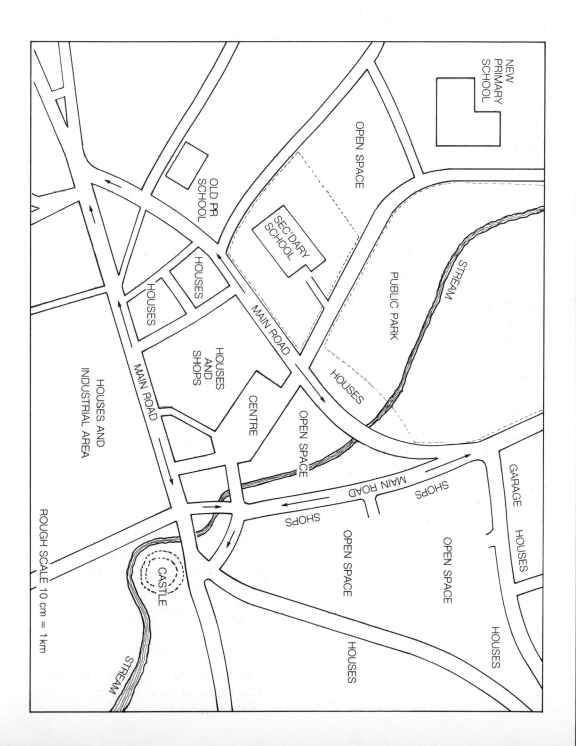

ROUGH SCALE 10 cm = 1km

NEW PRIMARY SCHOOL

OPEN SPACE

OLD PR SCHOOL

SEC'DARY SCHOOL

HOUSES

HOUSES

MAIN ROAD

HOUSES AND SHOPS

PUBLIC PARK

STREAM

HOUSES

CENTRE

OPEN SPACE

HOUSES AND INDUSTRIAL AREA

MAIN ROAD

MAIN ROAD

SHOPS

SHOPS

GARAGE

HOUSES

OPEN SPACE

OPEN SPACE

HOUSES

CASTLE

HOUSES

STREAM

Proposed Recreation Centre

1. Principally to house a theatre/concert hall, which can also be used for dancing or special events when seats are re-arranged.
A library, information centre, music, reading, conference and meeting rooms, together with a 'keep fit' gym and bar are planned for the ground floor.
First floor rooms are planned as games room, creche, local museum and rooms for hire by local organizations.

2. Virtually all the community, of all ages, can make use of it and enjoy its facilities.

3. It will be a new purpose-built structure to fit into the surrounding area and complement the town's style of buildings.

4. The site suggested is the open area of land between the main shopping centre and the stream.

5. This site is presently unattractive and would benefit from the development. It is also central and easy to get to, with room for landscaped gardens and plenty of room for parking.

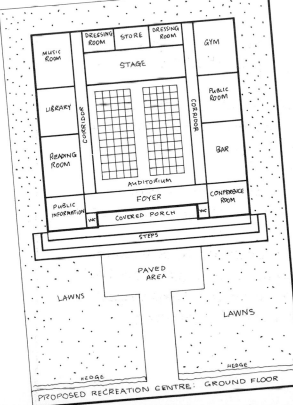

PROPOSED RECREATION CENTRE: GROUND FLOOR

Further Steps

A Ask someone in to judge the merits of the efforts so far – could be the head teacher.

B Bring in a Town Planner to talk about his work.

C Discuss the merits and demerits of the town and consider how it should develop.

D Ask groups at some point to present their ideas and to answer questions. You could chair this. You could have your judge in. You could have the class in role as townspeople, i.e. have a public meeting.

RECONSTRUCTIONS

Duplicate the plan and the questions. Have pencils and scrap paper ready.

1 The children need to be in 'planning groups' of four or so. Sit them round a table with the plan.

2 The background is that a village or settlement has vanished through time, leaving little evidence of what it was like. However, the attached plan exists – incomplete unfortunately. There is also evidence in an old book that, at its peak (and here I quote from the book):

3 'About 100 people lived and worshipped here, a peaceful people tending their sheep and cattle through the Summer and in the dark days spinning and weaving. They met in Summer beneath the spreading oaks – to gossip, to sing, to enjoy their festival. But in Winter round the roaring flames they would dance in the great barn.

'The children gathered by day to learn their letters, to count and recite from the Bible. Then on home-coming there was toil, family toil, for life was hard and all had to contribute.'

4 Can the planners reconstruct the village? It would be impossible to say, 'This is how it was', but you could say, 'This is how it might have been'.

5 Tell the children to draw upon the evidence, to follow the instructions, and to complete the plan either by using words, or by drawing.

6 The results can be displayed for comparison and for contrast.

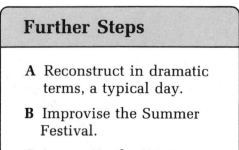

Further Steps

A Reconstruct in dramatic terms, a typical day.

B Improvise the Summer Festival.

C Improvise the Winter Festival.

DECISIONS

COPY

1 Where do you think the cottages were?

2 What do you think the dotted rectangle was?

3 Where were the spreading oaks? Draw some in.

4 Draw in the fields for the sheep and cattle.

5 There must have been a church. Where was it?

6 You can see the remains of an L-shaped building. What would you say it was?

7 There are two crossings to the river. One is a bridge. What might the other be?

8 There's a sort of grid. (It only shows up on aerial photographs.) What is it, do you think?

9 What else do you think would have been in the village? Write or draw it in. I think there must have been a blacksmith's shop for instance. What else?

DECISIONS

Here's the Plan

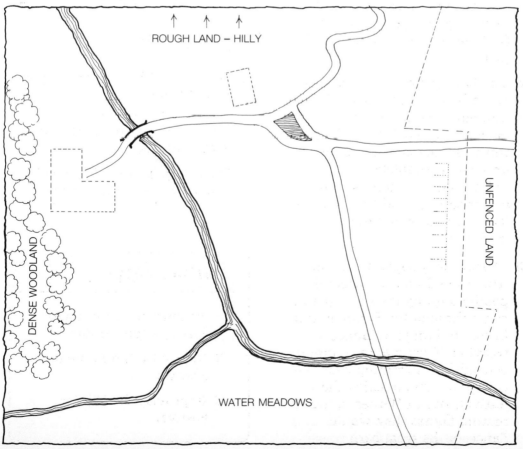

Persuasion

Age range: 8+
Time: 20 minutes
Aim: To practise and to resist persuasion

1 Ask the children: 'Can you think of anyone who has to persuade people in his or her job?'

2 Discuss this question with them. Perhaps introduce a few situations which involve persuasion, e.g. old person to accept help, father to try a new food, the baby to eat up his dinner.

3 Split the class into pairs, preferably in a good space and where you can make a noise.

4 Tell the pairs to be A and B. Tell them you are going to give them a situation and they are to act it out as soon as you say 'Go', and stop when you say 'Stop'.

5 Always keep to the same format, e.g.

'A is the shopkeeper, B is the customer. The shopkeeper is trying to sell you a rather old-fashioned pair of shoes.'

GO → → → → → **STOP**

'B is the shopkeeper, A is the customer. You are trying to get your money back on a faulty toy.'

GO → → → → → **STOP**

6 Discuss success and failure in terms of both parties. What phrases were used? Were any lies told? And so on.

You can think of your own situations. Even so, here are some, built around the theme of the adult and the child.

Possible Situations

a) 'Teacher says we should all have a computer.'

b) 'Everyone else gets to stay up till midnight.'

c) 'I don't see why I can't come home from the disco myself.'

d) 'Nobody has a bike as old as mine.'

e) 'They'll all laugh if I wear that to school.'

f) 'Can't I do my homework on Sunday?'

g) 'I'm fed up with the Guides/Scouts/Music Lessons. Can I leave?'

Further Steps

A Take one or two situations and extend them – suggesting moods, characters, persuasive language and so on.

B Ask pairs to prepare a short persuasive talk on a serious subject, e.g.

to join a group or club
to contribute to a charity
to take up a particular hobby

C Hear one or two talks. From each pair, one might give the talk while the other introduces, handles questions and concludes with thanks.

WORK PLACES

TEA BREAK OVER... BACK TO WORK!

SUPERVISOR

Be sure you have a large space available.

1 Discuss types of places where people work. List those likely to be reasonably familiar to all, and choose one for role-play e.g.

hospital	restaurant
building site	supermarket

2 Who is involved? Discuss and suggest roles.

What do they do? Discuss and then ask the role-players to tell you what they do.

How do they do it? Get role-players to show aspects of their jobs.

3 Who works with whom?

Who works for whom?

Who gives the orders?

→ Get small role-plays organised to show aspects of work on site involving co-operation

Plan with the class the layout of the site: workmen's hut, the office, construction, brick stack, sand, and so on.

4 Ask pupils to show you where they will start their action, by taking up positions.

Make a picture of the action. (A starting tableau)

5 Bring it to life on an agreed signal. It helps if you take a role, especially one which enables you to organise events within the improvisation e.g. site supervisor.

6 Stop the action. Discuss what has happened, and how a second run would yield better results. Suggest incidents that might happen and ask pupils to include some of them.

SITUATIONS & ROLE-PLAY

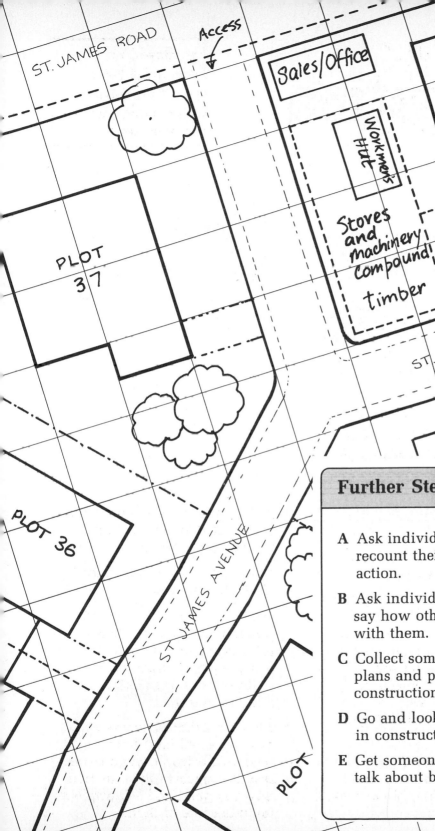

ST. JAMES ROAD

Access

Sales/Office

SHOWHOUSE

Workmen's Hut

PLOT 37

Stores and machinery compound

timber | sand and gravel | bricks | cem

ST. JAMES CLOSE

PLOT 36

ST. JAMES AVENUE

PLOT

Further Steps

A Ask individual pupils to recount their part of the action.

B Ask individual pupils to say how others interacted with them.

C Collect some tools, building plans and pictures of construction work.

D Go and look at a building in construction.

E Get someone to come and talk about building.

SITUATIONS & ROLEPLAY

Animation

You need a space and a few items of furniture, though the latter is not essential. Also a variety of pictures.

THE HEAD GIRL...

Further Steps

A Groups show what happened when the characters stepped out. This can be done in mime if preferred.

B Then introduce a prop or two. These can be improvised.

C Do the same for 'stepping in'. That is, what were the people in the picture doing before they made the picture?

1 Get the children to talk about pictures: from art galleries, magazines, posters, comics and so on.

Tell them to make small groups of no more than three.

Show them one or two pictures which seem to cover the interests of both sexes.

2 Tell the children you want them to bring a picture of their choice to life.

Give the groups time to discuss and experiment with their ideas on what happens when the people in their picture 'step out'. In other words, they take on roles and act out a situation.

Emphasise trying it out, rather than simply discussing it.

Proverbs

Ensure you have ample space to work in.

Further Steps

A Compile a longer list of proverbs.

B Ask the children to write a short dramatic situation in which a proverb is used at some point. This might be done in groups and then passed to another group to act out.

1 Talk to the children about proverbs in general: elicit how many they know.

Do we use them any more?
What was their purpose?
Discuss.
Penny wise, pound foolish
Out of sight, out of mind
Absence makes the heart grow fonder
A stitch in time saves nine
Nothing venture, nothing gain
Ignorance is bliss
Every cloud has a silver lining
It never rains but it pours

2 Take one as an example.

What does it mean?
Can we think of a situation in which it would apply?

3 Take that situation, put the pupils into groups of 3 or 4 and ask them to act it out.

4 Bring them together, and talk about the various interpretations. Show one or two if time permits and the children are willing.

5 Groups choose one to act out. The class have to decide what it is.

SITUATIONS & ROLE PLAY

99

WHAT'S IT ALL ABOUT?

Cover the names and photocopy the script for each group, or preferably each child.

Pencils will be needed.

1 Form groups of three, each to have pencils and script(s).

   Explain that the script has three people in it, that you want the group to decide who they are, what they are doing, and where. You want the speeches sorted out, and the characters given names.

2 Groups now set to work with help as necessary from you.

3 There can now be discussion of the various solutions.

   The process is the important thing.

Further Steps

A Act out the scene.

B Extend the scene, either by writing it, or improvisation.

COPY

What's It All About?

Possible
trio

BILL	Hey!
TOM	What?
BILL	Come and look.
TOM	I can't see anything.
BILL	You'll have to lean over.
TOM	No fear.
BILL	You have a look then.
SAM	Me?
BILL	Yes. Come on.
SAM	It makes me feel giddy.
BILL	Oh! For goodness' sake. Hurry up!
TOM	I'll hold your legs.
SAM	Well – don't let go.
TOM	'Course not, don't be daft. I'm not going to let you go. O.K.?
BILL	Do you see it?
SAM	I can't see anything. I'm dizzy. Pull me back.
TOM	What did you see anyway?
BILL	Don't tell. You have to see for yourself.
TOM	You could go down backwards.
SAM	Oh aye, and go right down to the bottom.
TOM	I'll have a go then. Hold my ankles – both of you.
BILL	That bush, the one with the spiky leaves. See it?
TOM	With the hole beside it?
BILL	Yes.
TOM	What about it?
BILL	Just keep looking.
SAM	Hurry up, we can't hold your legs much longer.
BILL	Oh, pull him back then.
TOM	What was it anyway?
BILL	I'll tell you – I might as well've told you in the first place.

Complaints

Age range: 10+
Time: Up to an hour
Aim: How to make complaints (when justified)

One table. A chair for each pupil. A few toys.

Write on blackboard –

i)   **Child buys toy in shop.**
ii) **Child takes toy home.**
iii) **Child finds it won't work.**
iv) **Child takes it back to shop.**

1 *Explain:*

That you yourself will be the shopkeeper.
That each child might be the child to begin with.
That each child might be the shopkeeper later on.

2 Set yourself up with table and toys and invite a child to be the customer.

Role-play the transaction.

Now tell the children that they should keep in mind what has just occurred.

Invite the child to return with the toy and tell the shopkeeper that it doesn't work.

Note:

There are many ways in which you as shopkeeper can manipulate events by being aggressive, accusatory, threatening and so on, but remember that your aim is to help the child deal with a situation many of us find tricky and many of us avoid. So give all the help you can within your role.

3 Discuss (out of role) what happened, what might have happened, what was forgotten, best avoided, and so on. Study the language used, and the mood of the complaint. If it succeeded, why? If not, why not?

4 Invite someone who has role-played the customer to go behind the counter. You can now join the class as observer. Another child becomes the customer.

I'LL REPLACE IT!
I'LL REPLACE IT!!

Further Steps

A Discuss with class the broad question of making complaints: your complaint might be personal (like a poor pair of shoes) or it might affect a lot of people (e.g. a dangerous crossing for young children and old folk).

B Devise a role-play in which an adult makes the complaint:

  i A parent complains that the surroundings of the school are littered with crisp packets and sweet papers. (Who would the other person be?)

  ii Someone complains to the police that a great number of motorists are not giving way at the crossing.

Age range: 10+
Time: 20/30 minutes
Aim: To foster visual and group awareness

The Photograph

A space in the classroom and perhaps a few photographs of groups of people.

1 Ask the children if they've been to any event where photographs were taken. You would probably get: school photographs, weddings, sports events and so on.

2 Ask the children if they can remember any details from the photographs they've seen of big occasions, topical events and so on.

3 Now that you have stirred their visual memory tell the children you are going to 'make' a photograph and ask them for ideas.

List the subjects of photographs the children suggest e.g.

The Wedding: 'Toasting the bride'
Football Match: 'The kick-off'

Then choose one.

4 Give every pupil a number. Tell them that when their number is called they go into the photograph in any role they choose, so long as it doesn't cut across anyone else's choice (e.g. only one bride is allowed!).

5 Call the numbers until you feel enough are in the photograph. (Keep a check on which numbers you call.)

6 Repeat the process with other subjects, ensuring that each child is included. After several photos have been assembled, mix them together one by one.

7 Possibilities for this are unlimited.

CRIME AND PUNISHMENT

Age range: 11+
Time: 1 hour
Aim: To bring a script to life

SITUATIONS & ROLE-PLAY

Have the scripts duplicated.
Pens or pencils will be needed.

Your classroom will do, but, because of noise level, a larger space will be better.

1 Issue the script once you have arranged groups of three or so, and tell the pupils to work on it in any way they want.

2 After a while, stop everyone and see what is happening. Then tell what you want done in specific terms.

Find out
– who the characters are/how many/name them

– what the situation is

Tell them at this stage not to change or add to the script, but to write in the characters and to cast them in their group. Help as necessary.

Once they've done that, tell them to act it out.

3 Stop the action to get feedback.

Further Steps

A Write or improvise the next scene in the existing group.

B Write or improvise the previous scene as a group.

C Discuss the various 'solutions', their pros and cons once groups have acted out their scene.

D Discuss the issues raised by the script.

The Script

What's up with you?

I don't see why we should all be punished.

Well, it's not much of a punishment is it?

Being kept in? For a week, when you haven't done anything.

I don't see why we should all get into trouble. Especially as we know who did it.

Careful!

Well, we do.

I know, but who's going to tell him to own up?

Not me.

Me neither.

He's too big.

If we all ganged up –

No. That's not fair.

It's not fair we're all going to have to stay in school just because someone else nicked some money.

Anyway, we don't know who did it – not really know. For sure, do we?

He's done it before.

I fell off a wall before. I suppose that means I shall do it again?

Oh, very funny!

I feel sorry for him.

Sorry? For him? Nobody likes him.

No. That's right. His dad doesn't either. If his dad thought he'd done it he'd be furious.

Yes. If his dad gave him decent pocket money he wouldn't steal other people's.

Why don't we just tell the head teacher when no one else is around?

That stinks.

I was just testing.

So what do we do?

Starters

Pass It On

All sit in a circle. An imaginary object has to be passed on. It must be passed on to someone other than your neighbour. As you hand it on, you say, 'It's jelly' or 'It's glue' or 'It's slimy'. It has to be carried accordingly, and again it changes: 'It's hot', 'It's greasy', 'It's sharp' and so on.

Port and Starboard

A riotous game to fill two minutes and exhaust the children. Agree port, starboard, amidships, stern and bow. As you shout directions they rush to fulfil them. Of course, the more you confuse them the greater the success.

Connections

Seated in a circle, children add a word to the one given by the previous speaker. If the connection seems very remote, a challenge may be made. You might get a sequence such as: red fire heat cooking kitchen mother car. 'Car' could produce a challenge.

Lucky Dip

Provide a box of objects, accessories, materials, hats, etc. Number the class. Whenever you call a number that child makes a lucky dip and has to utilise what comes up in mime, dance or drama.

Optimist/Pessimist

Here's a warming up game. Children pair off, and then decide who is the optimist, and who the pessimist. On the word 'Go' they converse. The optimist's sentences might always begin with 'Fortunately', and the pessimist's 'Unfortunately'.

What You Make It

Take any available object, a chair for example, and place it in the centre of the circle made by the class, who are seated. Either work on numbers called at random or make the 'next one in' the child who guesses the previous mime. The child in the centre uses the chair as something else, e.g. a bag of coal, a barrow, a television set, a sandwich board.

Leading

A simple pairs game which can do for 'trusting' goes as follows:

The leader guides the led anywhere round the room making the tour as interesting as possible. From time to time the leader guides the hand(s) of the led to touch surfaces and shapes.

The led is blindfolded or has eyes shut. After a while the journey stops, and the led repeats it, telling the leader what things were touched.

Where necessary, corrections are given.

The Minister's Cat

This is an old parlour game, but none the worse for that. It gives exercise in listening, speaking and vocabulary building.

With children unaccustomed to it begin by accepting any adjectives, e.g. The minister's cat is a grey/old/fat/greedy cat. Thereafter make it alliterative, e.g. The minister's cat is a monster/mangy/magnificent (or) lazy/long/laughable cat.

Physicals

Experiments with Paper

A piece of paper is passed from child to child. Each child must try to produce a different sound from the paper without tearing or otherwise destroying it. An advance on this would be for all the children watching and listening to say quietly a word which is thought to match the sound. These words can be recalled, put into a word bank, or other contexts.

Let's Go

Let's go to – circus, park, high street, airport, railway station, zoo etc. This can be handled as a linear event, with (usually) young children responding to the events built into the teacher's story.

It can move further if children are asked to supply any one part of the locale. This can be as individuals or in groups. The place can then be brought to life and given some shape and structure.

It can be more precise, or make more demands on everyone if a time is given, e.g. dawn on the high street, V.I.P. arrival at the airport, seeing off the 10.00 Inter-City express.

Forgotten Games

Games of parlour, street and playground could be the subject of book research and of asking old folk. When you've collected them and are proficient in them, why not teach the class next door. Hall or playground would do.

Discussion could reveal why some games have been lost, and how some survive.

Mime Tasks

Agree on environments: the library, the supermarket, the sports centre. Ask children to take one action only, and repeat it. This must be an action carried out within the chosen environment, e.g. stamping a book, stacking a shelf, hitting a ball. The actions can be shown half-class at a time.

Then in groups of three or so develop each action with a before and after into a sequence. Aim for selection of significant mime, for bold movement, and clear-cut sequence.

It should then be possible to arrange some of the contributions into a 'scene' depicting the chosen location.

Looking after . . .

This is a comprehensive term which can embrace things animate and inanimate, e.g. looking after the baby/the cat; the garden/the town; oneself/one's clothes . . . Methods obviously will vary, but there is a good chance here to report on a given form of looking after, to show through visual aids or first hand.

A structure to follow could be:

How we look after . . .

Why we look after . . .

How we feel about looking after . . .

Work Songs

Songs of the factory, field and sea are robust and authentic, and so give splendid chances to the children to combine vigorous singing, powerful movement, and clear speech.

The links with history offer further possibilities.

The Elements

Earth, air, fire, water provide a basis for a movement session, each being taken as a separate entity, then combining either in opposition, or as complementary. There is a great opportunity to devise your own 'sound track', or to use atonal music or electronic sound. Also there is scope for making and wearing simple, abstract or symbolic costume.

Stories

The Senses

Senses of sight and hearing are frequently used as stimuli. Bring in touch, smell and taste if possible as stimuli. Discussion can then follow on likes/dislikes in all three; situations in which children have experienced pleasant/ unpleasant sensations; things they avoid or are attracted to. Role-play could be developed on this basis.

For example:

The potholers feeling their way back to the surface in darkness.

The smells of the farm, the chemist's shop, the hospital ward.

Identification

A circle of children. Child in the centre says, 'I'm thinking of . . . ' and begins to describe someone sitting down, giving away as little as possible until the right answer is given. Wrong answer bears a penalty, right answers mean next one in the centre.

What is described need not be the children. It can be agreed that descriptions are of things in the school, in the town, of famous people, of television programmes, and so on.

Names

This is essentially discussion work, the object being to consider names, their meanings, connotations, associations and so on, and as it were to savour them.

Possible starters are –

first names
surnames
place names
foreign names
funny names
names we like/dislike

Dialect

Collect dialect words and phrases from your district. Put them on tape. Make a glossary. Organise a quiz (Mastermind?) to see who knows most.

Write a group script of short duration which contains the dialect. Act it out or tape it.

Stories/Telling

Sources for story-telling:

History, Bible, Sagas, Myths, Legends, Folk, Fables, Moralities

Tall stories, nonsense stories, fantasies, cautionary tales all have a place. Sometimes read or tell the story and leave it at that. Sometimes discuss it, sometimes invite active responses in drama or visual terms.

Descriptions

A great deal of work on description can be based on the simple framework:

What can be seen

What you've just seen

What you recollect

For example, the vase on your desk in full view: a vase observed, studied, then put away and immediately described; that vase, having been in the cupboard for a week, is described.

The unchanging nature of the vase is very much simpler than changing phenomena, so lead on to descriptions of the sky in different moods, to the seasonal changes seen from the classroom and to people in action and interaction.

Stories/Making up

(a) Work in groups of 6–8. Number round. Give a starting number, and a title, e.g. The Sad Story of the Mad Mouse. When you say start (and state clock, or anti-clockwise) each child adds a word as the story progresses.

There are ways you can help the structure as you try different stories:

Use direct speech

Start a new sentence

Add a simple action (seated)

Ask groups to tell others what their story was.

(b) For more experienced groups, here are some variations:

1 Add a phrase.

2 Add a phrase as it occurs, and not in a pre-arranged number order. But not two phrases or more consecutively.

3 Don't choose a title. See where the story takes you.

Hesitation/Repetition

Based on the radio game, form groups of four or so, and ask one of the class to hold a stop-watch, and another to choose the subject. Agree the length of time each subject is to run, e.g. 30 seconds. Number round the group 1–4, or 1–5. Explain that whoever starts the topic can be challenged for hesitating or repeating. If the challenge is successful he or she takes over the talk. If unsuccessful, the original speaker continues.

Explain procedures and begin. 'Number 4 to begin, and the subject is aircraft!' (Chosen by child from a list.) After 30 seconds (or agreed time) child with stopwatch says 'Stop'. Allow informal discussion about what went on. Continue. Remember, it's for enjoyment.

Questions and Answers

Leadership

An expedition is to make a trek across the Sahara. Members of the group will be selected from youngsters of both sexes.

A leader has to be appointed. What qualities, skills and experience should he/she have?

1 Write an advertisement inviting applications.

2 Work out what you would ask if you were to interview an applicant.

3 Work out what you would say if you were an applicant to be interviewed.

4 Role-play interviews.

5 Discuss leadership.

Who Uses?

Collect and display a number of artefacts which are reasonably easily recognised as used in the workplace or the home. Pair the children off. As far as possible allow them to choose their object.

Ask them to devise a situation which will show who uses it, how it is used, and what it is used for in the present instance. Extend the work. It is possible that some uses will interlock with others, so groups can join up to show that. Ensure that the name of the tool, the craft or calling and the user are known, e.g. a paint scraper, decoration, painter/decorator.

Who Says?

List a number of easily recognisable sayings, and then ask children to form groups and then supply a context in which the saying is used. This would be improvised.

Develop further by extending the improvisation into: before and after the event, to include more people, and so on.
Here are one or two examples of sayings:

Excuse me officer.

Are you being attended to?

Sorry sir, that's off the menu today.

Say 'Ah'.

Open wide.

EXCUSE ME OSHIFER

Openings

Looking at . . .

A work of art, e.g. statue or picture.

Help the children to observe, to refine their comments, to be open-minded, and to move beyond 'I like' and 'I don't like'. For example, without using highly technical terms, the teacher can introduce composition, structure, form, materials, size, texture, colour, movement and relationships.

Ask children to bring a photograph, poster, picture etc. they would like to talk to the class about.

Costume

Full costume for classroom work is impractical. Bits and pieces are not. For some children they help with starting. They also assist belief and characterisation, so have belts, collars, wrap-around materials, strips for trailing and so on. Hats can be very useful.

Abstract Themes

Words such as joy, sorrow, happiness, despair, anger, calm and so on can be used in various ways which are satisfying in themselves, and which help the children to grasp their deeper meanings.

It's possible to employ music, e.g. tone poems; poetry which creates mood, or directly expresses emotion, literature, or drama.

Music created by the children, or vocalising (e.g. keening or mouth music, sounds of a football crowd and so on) can be used. Above all because it best reveals the abstract, the use of the body in individual and group movement to express the word, should be of first importance.

Contexts might then be created, e.g. leaving, accusation, argument.

Magic and the Supernatural

Tell the children a story of magic or the supernatural. Ask them which parts they found exciting, fearsome and so on. In self-chosen groups give them time to dramatise excerpts or incidents. Tell the story again, this time as narrator, holding their action together.

Sound Patterns

From given sounds, sound sequences and sound patterns, pre-recorded, invite children to identify them and to give as much detail as possible. (BBC Sound Effects records are useful.) For example, wheels: wheels of barrow on gravel; car wheels on wet asphalt; train wheels; pram wheels on cobbles and so on.

This can be left purely as a listening and speaking exercise, or you might ask groups to produce a sound sequence of their choice, and reproduce it live for the class. Remind them what resources they have for this (vocal, percussion and so on). Have choices of your own in case some groups can't get started, e.g. the motorway slip-road.

Material

Provide a miscellany of remnants of e.g. cotton, velvet, hessian and so on. Make sure the materials have not been made up into a garment.

In small groups children work with any piece of material in instant improvisation.

On the word 'Change' they start another improvisation. On the words 'Change material' they do so and continue improvising.

History Based

Suppose you had covered 'The Plague' as a history patch or topic, the following activities would help the children grasp the nature and quality of the times:

1 Make up posies of herbs, and play out the rhyme, 'Ring a ring o' roses'.

2 Write a Proclamation which the Town Crier might have used.

3 Show how villagers outside London might have treated refugees from the capital.

4 Post up some extracts from Samuel Pepys's diary.

5 Discuss how the Plague might be dealt with today.

6 Imagine you are old, and came through the Plague when a child. Tell your story of that time to your grandchildren.

Limericks and Clerihews

Both forms lend themselves to fun and irreverence. The variations of content are numerous, and you can ask for last lines, first lines — indeed more or less anything goes so long as there is wit, enjoyment, and a grasp of form and metre.

Voices

Take a set of words, e.g. days of the week, months of the year, names from a directory, a list of cities, names of the teachers, etc.

What the groups then do is to arrange and speak the words, using all their voices solo or unison, to convey different emotions, which you will feed them, e.g.

'Say your words as though you are a gang plotting a bank raid.'

'You're apologising for breaking a window.'

and so on. Mostly the fun is for the group, but have some performance for the whole class.

Chorus

The basis of this is appreciating the flexibility of the human voice, and the musical quality of words.

Group the children in fives or sixes. Tell them to list words which sound ugly, angry, smooth, pleasant, soothing and so on. They will need help no doubt, so you might as a prelude to this show one or two such lists, or create a list with the children.

The idea now is to speak the words in any order with available voices, individual and group, so that when the final result is heard it expresses the key word (smoothly pleasant, etc.). It will be necessary to explain to the children that the words may be said with many or few or no repetitions.

Discuss rhythm, contrast, tempo and dynamics.

Story Based

Extracts from current class reading, or selected extracts from other work can be used to great advantage.

Clear-cut incident and character should be sought, also content which stimulates discussion on such things as beliefs and attitudes, in particular events and characters with whom children can identify or empathise.

The acting out is in a sense a revision of the book study. More than that, it helps to open up what lies beneath the text.

Decisions

The Expert

The child can often be the expert, e.g. on his/her hobby. There's a chance to give short talks, demonstrations and to deal with questions.

Help with structure might be needed, and also with the use of visual aids. You might use the opportunity to include an introduction.

Advertisements

Prepare and present advertisements either for known products, or for self-chosen ones: advertising their town as a place to visit, personal possessions as something to be desired, etc.

This might involve visual presentation, creation of images, dramatic use of voice, language of persuasion.

Making Plans

For a holiday or a party

For redecorating a room

For a new baby

For a birthday (Someone 100 years old?)

What is required when the choice is made, is a set of constraints which will impose conditions and create problems:

The party has a ceiling for money and numbers.

The room is for someone who likes a room to be unexciting.

The old lady is deaf and confined to her bed.

Applications

Perhaps you want to join a club, or enter for something. A letter might be desirable or necessary. Write it. A form might have to be filled in. Design it. You might be invited for an interview. Role-play it.

This process would be much richer if you could show good and bad examples of letters – forms which are obscure and forms which are clear. It would also benefit if discussion could turn upon 'Belonging' and its implications.

Rules

Draw up rules for a particular situation or place, e.g. rules for a sports day, for a youth club, for a museum or an historic house. Do this in groups of 3 or 4, then compare and contrast the results.

Devise and role-play, e.g. situations where rules have been infringed, or where the rules have to be explained or justified.

Special Occasions

Choose a special event – could be in the school year, in a pupil's life, a presentation, an overseas visitor.

Plan for the event, involving everyone, and carry it out.

A programme could be devised, and the whole thing seen as a 'rehearsal' for the real thing. This could be presented to another class.

People Who Work for Us

Interdependence has to be focused on here. There is ample opportunity to make this a topic, and within that opportunity to exercise the skills of interviewing, note-taking, reporting, or report writing, and role-play.

It should be possible to create a gallery of such people, or/and to show interdependence in diagrammatic form.

Health Topics

The purpose here would be unashamedly didactic – to show through discussion, role-play and dramatisation, what has probably been covered by other means elsewhere in the curriculum.

There is a chance to personalise and personify here, e.g. you could have a Mr Fixit, a Doctor Despair, a Nurse Knowall, Gertrude Glutton and Daniel Decay.

It should be possible to devise simple ways (and humorous ways) of pointing up the right way to health as contrasted with the wrong.

The Trial

This could be a revision of history e.g. Guy Fawkes, or it could be a nonsense accusation.

The charge against the accused is that he pleaded with his parents to give him less pocket money.

Allot roles and discuss procedures. Arrange classroom with the children. Run the trial.

Situations and Role-plays

Role-play

Handling social situations effectively e.g. making a complaint, airing a grievance, giving an apology, urging a course of action.

In analysing the role-plays, always draw attention to the 'other side' and always invite positive constructive comment on such things as courtesy, tone and the use of language.

Coping

Here the emphasis is upon getting it right, or doing something most efficiently:

mending a puncture

boiling an egg

turning right when cycling

The simulation can be accompanied by a present tense first person commentary: 'I'm turning my cycle on to its saddle.' Or it can be a present tense third person commentary: 'Now she's pulled into the centre of the road.'

Starters (1)

'Quickie' role-plays in twos or threes. Give a first line and designate the speaker, or allow who speaks first to start when the cue is given. Stop on command.

I just touched it, and it fell over.

Is this yours?

Where were you at five o'clock?

Starters (2)

A few developments can be brought in:

build in some action

introduce costume or props (simple ones)

create the previous scene

create the following scene

introduce (an)other character(s)

continue role-play and discussion.

Imaginary Environment

This is a 'free-wheeling' improvisation once started, so you will need to decide how much has to be pre-planned before the action begins.

You agree that the classroom, or working space is e.g. a castle battlement, a casualty clearing station, a sports arena, a dense forest, and so on.

What follows is subject to as much freedom as you feel able to give, but events should follow logically the original choice.

Script

Present an excerpt from the start of a script.

or

Present an excerpt from the middle of a script.

or

Present an excerpt from the end of a script.

Group the children according to the number of characters you expect to be in the script. Ask groups to work out the script, by using talking, writing, reading and acting. You might suggest a length, either by time or by number of pages.

Start

I don't like the look of him, do you?

He's hanging around again.

Yes. Every night as it gets dark. You'd wonder why.

He gives me the shivers.

Middle

And this is our oldest inhabitant, Mrs Ferguson.

No, please don't get up, Mrs Ferguson.

You're very kind.

End

You mean it wasn't him anyway?

No. He wasn't even there.

That explains it then.

Let's Be . . .

the new boy, the stranger, the learner, the hero, etc.

Once these have been agreed, make them the centre of a piece of role-play. This might be the time to take one and work out a scenario, so that to begin with, everyone has agreed common ground, greater security, and a chance in acting out to show variations.

Lesson notes

Use these pages to jot down
some of your own ideas